Survival Handbook for Young Pastors

*Keys to Overcoming Seven Imposing
Battlefields of Pastoral Ministry*

Dr. Robert S. Miller

Survival Handbook for Young Pastors
Keys to Overcoming Seven Imposing
Battlefields of Pastoral Ministry
by Dr. Robert S. Miller

Printed in the United States of America

ISBN 978-1-60647-977-3

Unless otherwise indicated, Bible quotations are taken from *The Holy Bible: Today's New International Version* (TNIV). Copyright © 2005 by International Bible Society.

Illustrations throughout book: Phil Bruner
Cover Illustration: Phil Bruner
Cover Design: Brian McCloskey
Photo of author: Danielle Saletta
Editing: Lucinda Sutton

Statistics on the back cover are provided by Focus on the Family, The Fuller Institute, George Barna, and Pastoral Care Inc.

www.xulonpress.com

"Robert Miller's *Survival Handbook for Young Pastors* is a must read, not only for those entering ministry but for all who are trying to find their way and God's way in the turbulent territory of ministry in our time. Biblically grounded, theologically perceptive, experientially authentic and practically engaged, Miller's work is a treasure chest of wise counsel, creative insights, passionate appeals and provocative challenges that have the power to transform your ministry. Coming from the heart, mind and experience of a seasoned pastor, this manual provides invaluable insights and tools that should be, but all too often are not, essential elements in the preparation of persons for ministry."

— Manfred T. Brauch, Professor Emeritus of Biblical Theology, Palmer Theological Seminary and author of *Hard Sayings of Paul* and *Abusing Scripture: The Consequences of Misreading the Bible*.

"A disciple's faith, a pastor's heart, a veteran's experience, and a wise and caring man's passion converge on the pages of this 'manual' intended for new pastors. Engaging yet pointed, direct while still positive, Miller makes his point that to survive — and thrive — in ministry requires that paradoxical blend of our best effort and God's abundant grace."

—Dr. Peter Schreck, Marriage and Family Therapist

"*Survival Handbook* is a practical manual that goes beyond the textbook ministry issues which Christian workers are trained for in Bible school or Seminary. It tackles the real spiritual dynamics of life and ministry head-on. Dr. Miller takes a solid Biblical theology of ministry and then shows us in very concrete terms how to walk that out in the trenches of ministry. This book clearly identifies the underlying issues of the challenges of full-time ministry and then gives practical Scripture-centered strategies on how to overcome – how to live the life that God offers us and more abundantly.

This book is not only for those in pastoral ministry; it is equally relevant to those serving in cross-cultural missions since the material is focused on our identity in Christ, a balanced view of the battle we face and practical, biblical strategies for the challenges. Dr. Miller writes '*If God has called you to minister in the desert, God will create a stream in the desert to quench your thirst and give you strength.*' I believe this book will take you down the path that leads to that stream. Every full-time Christian worker needs to be familiar with the strategies presented in this book. I will certainly be giving it to every member of my team."

> —Joanna Beske, team leader/ missionary in Senegal, West Africa

"I wish I'd had Robert Miller's *Survival Handbook for Young Pastors* in my back pocket when I entered into professional ministry. The survival keys here can surely prevent years of pain, confusion, and ineffectiveness. This book was not written in an ivory tower. On the contrary, one can tell right off the bat that a real, on-the-ground pastor, who himself has gone through many battles, wrote it. Packed with wisdom and practical skills, this book can surely help pastors—young or old—to keep their eyes on the prize and to genuinely minister to people in Christ's name."

> —F. Albert Tizon, PhD, Asst. Professor of Evangelism & Holistic Ministry, Palmer Theological Seminary, and author of *Transformation after Lausanne* and *Linking Arms, Linking Lives*

Prologue

Imagine a battlefield scenario. A small group of soldiers gather in a secure place for a few hours before heading back to the front lines. There is no time for pleasantries. Rather, every minute is filled with key, strategic discussions. Each soldier listens carefully, knowing that such information might be the difference between life and death.

Take what you read in this book and place it within that context. The main presupposition of this work is that the battle in ministry is real. Pastors today are undoubtedly in the midst of deadly spiritual combat. If not careful, they will be destroyed. Those who are committed to advancing the Kingdom of God are in the cross hairs of the enemy.

Every year, hundreds of Bible College and Seminary graduates enter into the foreign and dangerous terrain of full-time ministry. Some are familiar with the principles of spiritual warfare, but many are not. Not all understand the dynamics of power and authority structures, or are able to endure intense criticism. Few know how to establish and maintain healthy boundaries.

Nearly everyone enters their ministry context with glaring blind spots such as these. This is true in any profession, but in ministry the spiritual battle is so persistent and intense that one mistake can be lethal. The combat zone is not the place to practice military exercises for the first time (without careful supervision). Yet thousands of young pastors and missionaries march bravely into combat just this way, some not even aware the enemy is trying to pick them off.

Imagine a soldier entering into combat with every piece of standard issue equipment except a gas mask. That soldier may be the best marksman in his unit, but because of a lack of equipment, he is dangerously susceptible to biological and chemical agents.

It is not simply a matter of gifting. It is also a matter of equipping.

I do not intend to be melodramatic when I speak of surviving in ministry. Many gifted pastors fall. Though no one knows the exact figure, one source estimates that 1500 pastors and ministry leaders in North America step away from their post every month due to conflict, burnout, or moral failure.[1] Half of the pastors starting out in ministry do not last beyond five years.[2] Clergy counselor Rowland Croucher suggests that the numbers of ex-pastors roughly equal that of serving clergy throughout the Western world.[3]

Do you hear their voices? Have you heard their stories?

"I have been in ministry in one way or another for over twenty years. What surprised me the most, hurt me the greatest, and frequently caused me to reassess my call was the wounding caused by "friendly" fire from within the church which came from co-workers, friends, and members of the congregation alike. No one warned me about this dimension in ministry, that it would be my greatest challenge and my greatest pain."
—Associate Pastor of an independent, non-denominational church

"As I reflect on thirty-five years of ministry, I realize that many of my former colleagues are no longer pastors...The attrition rate has been high and the cost to souls is astronomical. The majority of my acquaintances simply encountered such turmoil and situational

conflict that they felt they could not continue
to pastor. Too often, they had no friend or
accountability group to share their pain or
provide emotional or spiritual support. Many
well-meaning Christians in their congregations
ignored the signs of 'battle fatigue.' Instead,
congregations overwhelmed my pastor
friends with unrealistic expectations, negative
criticism and misplaced anger." —Pastoral
staff member, Focus on the Family.[4]

"I had no understanding of the politics of
the church. In fact, I did not want anything
to do with church politics. I entered ministry
because I felt called to help others. I was
young and naïve. I did not understand that
every decision would be characterized as a
choosing of sides, or as aligning myself with
some subgroup that struggled for power
within the church. I had no clue of the depth
of isolation and loneliness that I would
experience within the community of faith
because I tried to do what I believed was
right." — Angel

"I was unprepared for the insidious behind-
the-scenes coalition-building that suddenly
occurred in my congregation. Some key
members began to gossip, slander, and share
half-truths in order to convince other members
to stand in opposition against me. These

power plays 'in the name of God' brought me close to resigning." — Anonymous

"Early on in my ministry, a deep discouragement settled on me. I felt deserted by a number of people. I felt overwhelmed by the number of situations that had arisen that I had no answers for. I did not handle the rejection of certain people well. I was frustrated by my lack of ability to measure myself and my performance. I never knew when I was done, or if I was doing a good job, or if my priorities were accurate. I found that I did not enjoy the fishbowl of ministry. I am a private, quiet, reserved person and I realize that a senior position was probably not what I was created for." — Michael, sixteen years after leaving the ministry

Though the number of disheartening testimonies from pastors and ex-pastors seems to be growing at an exponential rate, the harsh relational terrain of ministry has existed for thousands of years. Jesus was misrepresented (Lk.11:15-20), rejected (Jn.1:11), betrayed by a co-worker (Lk.22:47-48), disowned by a close companion (Mk.14:66-72), falsely accused (Mt.26:59-60) and deserted by His friends when He needed them the most (Mt.26:36-46). The Apostle Paul dealt with many of the same challenges. Our Lord warns us, "No servant is greater that his master. If they persecuted me, they will persecute you also"

(Jn.15:20). We must prepare for these challenges if we are to survive.

This book is organized around seven primary words that I wish I had heard at the beginning of my ministry career—seven words that speak to seven imposing battlefields in pastoral ministry. I do not claim to offer a final word on any of these topics. In fact, I hope and pray you will want to learn more about each of them, and where possible I've tried to point you in the right direction. A survival guide, by definition, is concise and zeroes in quickly on the urgent, laying the groundwork so that one day you can think well beyond surviving to thriving in the ministry to which you have been called. It is my hope that by passing this advice to you now, you will be able to realistically assess the challenging and adventurous terrain that stretches out before you. Lift up your eyes and look upon this land! It is a land filled not just with danger, but with great opportunity.

This handbook is my offering to you, and not for mere survival, but for victorious, anointed service to the King of Kings, Jesus Christ.

Table of Contents

Survival Key #1:   Know Your God
Thousands of pastors have lost their way by trying to minister in their own strength, only to find themselves burned out and without motivation to go on. Apart from intimate fellowship with the Lord, there is no chance of survival.

Survival Key #2:   Know Yourself
Over 3000 churches in America shut their doors annually. A strong sense of identity and a formidable reservoir of inner courage are required if a pastor is to survive the complex and intense world of ministry.

Survival Key #3:   Know Your Enemy
Casual mindsets about the strategies and traps of the enemy have led many pastors to the brink of destruction.

On the last and greatest day of the Festival, Jesus
stood and said in a loud voice, "Let anyone who is
thirsty come to me and drink. Whoever believes in
me, as Scripture has said, rivers of living water will
flow from within them."
John 7: 37-38

Survival Key #1
Know Your God

It was a gray, cloudy April morning in Canada. The children had gone to school, his wife to work. After a slow start to his morning, Pastor Rowland Croucher decided to do something he'd never done before. He turned the phone down, put a note on the front door, and went back to bed. He was burned out — and within two months, he resigned his pastorate.[5]

As I look back on those years, the progression away from intimacy with the Lord and toward obligatory pastoral service was very subtle. Seemingly small choices, daily decisions — the way I used my time and structured my life — eventually led me to a place of emptiness and despair. One morning, I awoke to find that the fire was gone. I was busier than ever in my church ministry, but I had lost my first love and was dying a cold, lonely death. — testimony of a self-proclaimed "burned out" pastor

So much of what I have learned about survival in ministry is based on the following statement: "Inward before outward, secret before public." You must win the battle within your own person if you are to survive in ministry. Success in this inner terrain requires a commitment of the heart and a renewing of the mind. Start your training here in the secret places.

Let the river flow into your heart.

There is a river that proceeds from fellowship with the Spirit, a river that waters your thirsty life. The flow of this river is dependent upon your heart's posture before the Lord. A subtle shift will cause the flow to pause or even stop. Without that life-giving river, your heart will become a desert.

There are times when we attempt to minister apart from this flow. Such a condition is so prevalent that we can become accustomed to it and think it is normal. After all, no one is perfect; we're all human. But the sobering truth is that a pastor who is preaching, leading a service, or counseling a congregant apart from abiding in the Spirit may as well be playing the role of a minister in a Hollywood film. We cannot give what we do not have. Without the living water, there is no living, vital ministry.

This survival key is in some sense the most important one of all, which is why it comes first. In fact, it can't be isolated from any of the other keys. The capacity to know yourself, your enemy, the terrain, and your mission, as well as your ability to respect boundaries and to lead effectively are inextricably tied to your relationship with God.

Everything is about the river. Is your heart alive or is it dead?

> *How long does it take for a heart to become an arid desert? Not years and not months. Guard your heart daily.*

How long does it take for a heart to become an arid desert? Not years and not months. Guard your heart daily.

The river of fellowship with your Lord and Savior is the key to your life and your ministry; everything else takes second place. This priority must be reflected in your daily schedule, in your weekly schedule, and in your yearly calendar.

The Daily Discipline

The very minute your eyes open for the first time in the morning, dedicate yourself to the service of the Lord. Before your feet touch the floor, before you rise from your bed, commit yourself to the Lord's purposes for the day.

Do not listen to people who say this special appointment with the Lord can occur anytime of the day. Do not rationalize by saying, "I'm not a morning person, so I'll have my time with the Lord in the evening." You *must* begin your day by being alone with God.

I schedule early appointments with people, but my first appointment is always with Jesus Christ.

I must spend time with Him. Not just five or ten minutes. I must linger with Him. I need the living water. I need to know Him and to be known by Him. If I forego this priority-one appointment, my heart will become a desert and I will die. When we forego our time with the Lord, we are choosing to take our eyes off the river of life and go our own way. It is both subtle and dangerous. No Christian can afford to lose this early morning battle. No pastor can lose sight of the significance of these early morning decisions.

Linger in the morning with your Lord. Though the Bible is an essential ingredient of this appointment with Jesus, this time is not about Bible study. Schedule other times in your day for the discipline of study. This time is about relationship. It is a time of friendship, of lingering.

I start this morning time on my knees. This position reminds me that Jesus is Lord (and I am not). Kneeling reminds me of my desperate need for my Savior's intervention in my life. I may read a psalm. Often I will read it out loud. I find that I need to get out of my head, break the silence, and use my voice and my body. I enter His courts with thanksgiving and praise. Do not be concerned about feelings. Emotional satisfaction will come and go. God will bless you for your consistency and your earnest desire to meet with Him. When we seek Him with all our hearts, He will be found by us (Jer.29:11-13).

After a time of kneeling, I often walk with Him. I go outside or even just move around the room. I have come to understand the simple truth that my physical body wants to get comfortable. I know how easy it is to be lulled into religious exercise and forget that I am actually meeting with a Person—the King of Kings!

In this regard, we are all the same. There is a dominion we must exert over our physical bodies if we are to become mature disciples of our Lord. "Run in such a way as to get the prize. Everyone who competes in the games goes into strict training. They do it to get a crown that will not last; but we do it to get a crown that will last forever. Therefore I do not run like a man running aimlessly; I do not fight like a man beating the air. No, I beat my body and make it my slave so that after I have preached to others, I myself will not be disqualified for the prize" (1Cor.9:24-27). Practice praying in the Spirit. Practice singing the new song to your Lord. Practice pouring yourself out for Him in praise and adoration.

Then practice listening. Ask the Lord to speak His heart to your heart. Give Him permission to shine His light in every area of your life. Pray this: "Whatever You desire to say, Lord—whether it is an encouragement, an exhortation, a prophecy or a rebuke—I want to hear it! I need to hear it!"

During such listening times, all types of distractions will come to you. Some of the distractions are external (the phone, the weather, a person passing by, a sound). However, the most persistent distractions are internal (looping thought cycles, the "to do" list of ministry, hunger pangs, carnal desires, feelings, boredom). Do not beat yourself up over these interruptions; this is simply the terrain where the battle will take place each morning. Don't despair! Realize that this indeed is the battle and that you can achieve a measure of victory in the name of Jesus!

Some days you will totally overcome distraction and find yourself in sweet fellowship with the Spirit. Other days, it will seem like an uphill battle from start to finish. You are being strengthened in both the easy and the hard times. Engage in fighting through the distraction. You are weight-lifting in the spiritual realm. Over time, your muscles will develop. God will give you power and teach you techniques to wait on the Lord (for this is what you are practicing daily). The daily workout causes you to become tenacious in your spirit. This is a rare characteristic among North American Christians. In our culture, if something is hard, we give up too easily. We need to learn from our brothers and sisters in the 3rd world and especially from those who are being persecuted for their faith. They are tenacious; they have learned how to stand in the storm. God wants you to be tenacious! The Holy Spirit is calling you to His daily training ground, teaching you perseverance.

Traditionally, in many Christian circles, this daily personal appointment has been called a "quiet time." Anyone who has walked with the Lord for an extended period of time knows that it is difficult to become quiet. It is a raging war, and the enemy wants you to grow weary in trying.

How would you design an important meeting with the most respected person in your life? You would eliminate as many distractions as possible. You would prepare for that meeting and do everything in your power to make the most of this special

opportunity. Have that mindset with your morning
appointment with Jesus.

The Weekly Discipline
Along with your daily quiet times with the
Lord, see that you have an extended time away in
the wilderness[6] every week. Practice solitude. Rise
early in the morning and don't return to your normal
routine until after lunch. Take only your Bible and
your journal. Find a secluded place where you can
hide away. It would be best if this place is away from
your home and away from the church. Or, better
yet, take a hike. Discover new secret places. Don't
worry if it is raining or cold. Consider Jesus in the
wilderness for forty days. Think about the millions of
brothers and sisters in the world today who are being
tortured daily because of their faith in Christ. You
can survive six hours in less than perfect conditions.
For too long, American Christianity has been
about breakfast meetings (sitting in comfortable
booths clutching our coffee cups), board rooms (planning new strategies for church growth) and conferences (listening to experts and then rushing to grab
the DVDs and the books). Our faith has been born
under artificial lighting and at a room temperature
of sixty-eight degrees. Many of us do not know the
feeling of the cold winter wind in our faces. We've
not had to walk for hours in the rain or gone without
food for a couple of days. We've become soft. I am
thankful for heat and air conditioning, but from time
to time it is essential for us to step out of the artificial.
Howard Macey points to this truth when he writes:

"The spiritual life cannot be made suburban. It is always frontier, and we who live in it must accept and even rejoice that it remains untamed."[7]

We need to get back to our roots. God calls us to the wilderness—to God's sanctuary. When I walk in the mountains, I become very aware of how big the mountain is and how small I am. I gain a deeper appreciation for the Mountain Maker. In nature, we can re-capture the wonder that has been lost under artificial lighting and controlled environment of automobiles, computers, and restaurants.

Words, written and spoken, surround us all the time. We are inundated with words, but are unfamiliar with, perhaps even intimidated by, silence. Mountains will speak, but with very few words. Meadows will sing, but with very few words. Nature knows how to bow before the Creator. Our artificial world is all about self-expression—all mouth and no ears.

You will be tempted to take a friend with you on these excursions. Fight that temptation. Your wilderness time is a training ground for you and the Holy Spirit. In these hours, you will experience a wrestling within yourself that exposes weakness and depletion. But while you are experiencing a variety of frustrating feelings, the Lord will be strengthening your ankles as you walk this trail. You are being trained and conditioned for battle. Through this discipline, you are learning to depend on God alone.

I have met only a handful of people who operate out of the Spirit's strength. The Spirit is delighted to fill every man and woman who is rightly postured before Him. The moment I begin to fuel my life with my own power, I have lost sight of the spiritual reality that apart from the Lord, I can do nothing (Jn.15:5). The morning battle and the weekly time away, when operating according to the Spirit, establish this truth deep within our souls and cause the river to flow from Him to us. When we find that sweet communion, much power is available for ministry

> *Nature knows how to bow before the Creator. Our artificial world is all about self-expression— all mouth and no ears.*

to others. Without this flow, we are like a broken water fountain in the park on a hot day—unable to offer what people really need.

The Discipline of Personal Retreats

Finally, I recommend that you get away for a personal overnight retreat at least four times a year (These should last at least 24 hours.) Keep it simple, remembering that this practice is not about luxury or comfort. It is about equipping. These disciplines frustrate the carnal nature and strengthen the spiritual nature, so don't be surprised if you feel like you're in a battle. You are.

Prepare for your personal retreats. Ask the Lord ahead of time, "What is it that you want me to consider? What is it that you're showing me about my heart, my family, my ministry?" Come to your retreat with a specific question for the Lord or a specific area of study. Consider also fasting during part or all of your personal retreats. The old proverb is true: "If you aim at nothing, that's precisely what you'll hit." So write down the purpose of your retreat. Of course, that purpose might and often does change. The Lord might lead you in a completely different direction. Be prepared for a new direction, but come prepared to make effective use of your time away. I believe the Lord appreciates our passion to discover and to ask.

You may be astounded by my emphasis on time alone with God. Why would so much of a pastor's time be given to the inward journey? What about other people? What about the "to do" list or the visits or the organization of the ministry? Just remember: Inward before outward; secret before public.

This is the example that Jesus set for us. The disciples often found Him spending time alone with His Abba on a mountain or in the wilderness. They watched Him depart for hours at a time or overnight, and then saw Him return refreshed and renewed in vision. If our Lord needed alone time with His Father, how much more so do we?

Inner reconciliation is a prerequisite to being an ambassador of reconciliation. In order to have something to give to people when you are with them, you must spend time alone in the river. You need to be "wet" with the Spirit when people brush up against you. They should be able to sense that you've been soaking in His Presence. Don't towel off! Don't make yourself "presentable." Drip His Presence on the floor of the kitchen, on the carpet of your office, and on the platform of your sanctuary.

I have set a basic structure before you that, if followed, can assist you in keeping communion with the Lord. Practice the classical spiritual disciplines consistently. View them not as taskmasters, but as allies in living out the abundant life that God desires for you. When operating according to the Spirit, they will enable the river to flow freely from Him to you to others.

Let the river renew your mind.

The river flowing from God's Word and God's Spirit must not just irrigate our hearts, but also our thinking. In his book, *The Three Battlegrounds*, Francis Frangipane reminds us that the blood of Christ Jesus was spilled at a place called "Golgotha," which means "the place of the skull." A fierce battle is still raging in the "place of the skull" (in the realm of our thoughts). We must win this battle by finding and putting to death all anti-biblical perspectives. The Bible tells us not "to be conformed to the pattern of this world," but to be transformed by the renewing of our minds (Romans 12:2).

How does the river (God's Word, God's Spirit) flow into our minds? Every piece of information that I retrieve must first pass through my "mind-skin"[8] (my personal system of adopted life paradigms). Every emotion, thought, imagination, conviction, etc. — is shaped and manipulated by this filter before I even begin consciously processing the information. If my mind-skin is not aligned to the Word of God, no matter how hard I try, I will not be able to enter into God's perspective concerning all that is going on inside me, around me, and in the world. But if I allow the Holy Spirit to pour over my mind-skin, the very way I *process* can be transformed and my mind can be renewed (properly aligned to the principles in the Word of God).

Some examples of mind-skin constructs:

- Some people see the glass half-full; others see it half-empty (regardless of which glass catches their eyes).
- Some people crave change; others fear it (regardless of the change that is occurring).
- Some, because of their past wounds, find it hard to trust people in authority. Others, because of their good experiences with authority figures, find it easier to trust (regardless of whether or not the present authority figure is trustworthy or not).

Our mind-skins are made up of unconscious patterns that we've adopted in order to make sense of the world and survive in it. We can remain in subjection to these unconscious patterns or we can cry out for God's river to pour over us.

When God's river flows into our mind-skins, a miracle begins to happen: our perspective changes even if our circumstances remain the same. When our mind-skins begin to align with God's principles, paradigm shifts begin to occur.

> *I can't* becomes *I can.*
> *It will never change* becomes *Anything is possible.*

Worthless becomes *Invaluable*.
Just getting by becomes *Aspiring and achieving*.

God's thinking is not at all like our thinking (Is.55:8). We see an acorn; He sees an oak tree. We see a closed box; He sees an open lid. We see our worthlessness; He sees our great potential in Christ.[9]

Jesus said, "No one pours new wine into old wineskins. If he does, the wine will burst the skins and both the wine and the wineskins will be ruined" (Mk.2:22). Is your mind-skin old and rigid or is it new and flexible? This is an important question because the way you *process* information can make or break your ministry.

Remember, every bit of information must first pass through your unconscious paradigm grid. If your mind-skin interprets disagreement as rejection, then you will see honest challenge as disaffirmation or betrayal. If your mind-skin interprets change as uncomfortable and frightening, then you will unconsciously struggle with change of any kind. If your mind-skin registers every conflict as a personal attack, you will distance yourself from every person with whom you share an argument.

Moving Forward

Is there a path to freedom? The transformation that we long for comes by the renewing of our minds. The Lord has a different perspective on things. We need His eyes. We need His way of thinking. Ask Jesus to transform the way you *process* information.

31

The rigid expectations that you and I have unconsciously adopted in order to survive must give way to new, flexible mind-skins. If we ask Him and if we are willing to do all He directs us to do, our Lord will gladly pour His river into us!

Those who listen to the word but do not do what it says are like people who look at their faces in a mirror and, after looking at themselves, go away and immediately forget what they look like.
James 1:23-24

Survival Key #2
Know Yourself

One of my personal struggles as a young man was living with a fear of failure. For most of my life I made decisions based on my ability to perform. If failure was a possibility I would find a reason not to try. This way of dealing with the possibility of failure continued as I grew older, and it affected my total approach to life—including ministry. I got rather good at masking the true excuse for my decisions by using logic that sounded spiritually reasonable. In fact, I was so good at it that I usually failed to recognize it and often called the decisions I made wisdom and an act of faith. The truth is that it was the wisdom of man and that my faith was captive to a huge calculator—one that wouldn't let me step into the realm of risk.

— David Crone, senior pastor of The Mission, Vacaville, CA[11]

There is a universal saying to the effect that it is when men are off in the wilds that they show themselves as they really are. As in the case with the majority of proverbs there is much truth in it, for without the minor comforts of life to smooth things down, and with even the elemental necessities more or less problematical, the inner man has an unusual opportunity of showing himself—and he is not always attractive. A man may be a pleasant companion when you always meet him clad in dry clothes, and certain of substantial meals at regulated intervals, but the same cheery individual may seem a very different person when you are both on half rations, eaten cold, and have been drenched for three days—sleeping from utter exhaustion, cramped and wet.

> —Kermit Roosevelt, son of Theodore Roosevelt[12]

"God is doing a work in me
He's walking through my rooms and halls
Checking every corner
Tearing down the unsafe walls
Letting in the light
And I am working hard,
To clean my house and set it straight. . ."

Help Me Be New, Sara Groves

Have you ever found yourself in a situation where, all of a sudden, you experience much more emotion than the context warrants? A moment before, everything was normal. But then, something happened and now raw feelings are flooding into the moment like a waterfall. What was it? A specific word? A particular facial expression? A subtle dismissal? What was the trigger and where did it send you?

In order to be liberated in our ministry to others, we must find a measure of liberation in our own selves. We must do the inner work, we must find the buttons, that when pushed, cause us to react instead of respond.

Survival key #2 is all about personal discovery. This battlefield requires great courage and perseverance. Are you willing to look into the mirror? Are you willing to ask the Holy Spirit to reveal the deep script written on the fabric of your heart? Proceed carefully and prayerfully in this terrain.

The Mirror

Pastors, we are extremely vulnerable to attack if we do not settle the issue of identity in the very core of our beings. We must deal with the mirror or it will destroy us.

God's desire is that every pastor learns:
*How to be self-identified
*How to withstand betrayal and rejection
*How to disagree with a co-worker and still remain active in fellowship with that person

*How to receive correction without being offended.

> **We must deal with the mirror or it will destroy us.**

The list could go on and on, but the main point is this: The Holy Spirit longs to establish a solid sense of self in every one of us. Talents, skills, charisma, and training are all wonderful tools for ministry, but if we have not graduated from the identity school led by the Spirit of God, then all our ministry efforts are built on sinking sand. God's identity classes are held every day. They are twenty-four hours long. All the classes are practicums. We learn by watching our Teacher and following His example.

Are you interested in this school? Are you teachable? Do you really want to learn? If so, you are welcome to enroll in God's school, and He will gladly be your Teacher.

During His earthly ministry, Jesus had a solid sense of self. Neither the people praising Him nor those cursing Him altered His view of Himself and His mission. How did He walk through life in this manner? What was His secret? His identity was grounded not in the way people looked at Him, but in the way His Father looked at Him.

God wants each of us to look into the mirror and see ourselves through His eyes. Of course, if our eyes are not opened to seeing Jesus present with us, the mirror will be haunting. I cannot tell you how

God will form your sense of self, but the following guidelines may prove helpful in the journey:

[1] We must surrender our lives entirely into the hands of our loving heavenly Father. We must build upon His promises and His love. A person's self-worth and identity cannot be built on the opinions of others.

[2] It is imperative to say "no" to any agenda besides allowing the river to flow through our lives into the world.

[3] Family of origin work is essential. Part of this work is learning about our unconscious contracts concerning trust, loyalty and love. It is imperative that we discover how our buttons get pushed, because, believe me, they will get pushed.

[4] Inner healing and deliverance is another essential area. The power to change is available in the name of the Lord Jesus. The Bible teaches that breakthroughs come by way of confession, repentance, taking back the ground in the Name of Christ and complete surrender to his Lordship. Any demonic strongholds in our lives must be destroyed in this manner—strongholds of resentment, pride, lust, envy. The enemy will capitalize on any advantage he can find in our past, our character, and our ways of relating to others.

Just as physical mirrors are used for the sake of external presentation, we need spiritual mirrors that reflect back to us our inner character and condition. These spiritual mirrors can emerge in various ways.

They may come as we are reading His Word or while we are praying. God may reveal them through the community of faith (a prophecy or a word of counsel from a friend) to bring us insight about ourselves. He may also use circumstances or other people to hold up a mirror to our faces.

A word of caution: Not all mirrors offer a perfect reflection, and often our eyes do not see clearly even when they do. Nevertheless, we must take courage to stand in front of spiritual mirrors when we are given the opportunity. God wants us to see our present condition so that when He changes us, we will rejoice all the more.

The Script

> And now for the first time I knew what I had been doing. While I was reading, it had, once and again, seemed strange to me that the reading took so long; for the book was a small one. Now I knew that I had been reading it over and over—perhaps a dozen times. I would have read it forever, quick as I could, starting the first word again almost before the last was out of my mouth, if the judge had not stopped me. And the voice I read it in was strange to my ears. There was given to me a certainty that this, at last, was my real voice.
> —C.S. Lewis, *Till We Have Faces*[13]

> *In the name of Jesus, set your natural script before the cross and ask the Lord to place in your heart the prophetic script He has written for you.*

There is a script hidden deep in every person's heart; it is one's life story told from a personal perspective. It is composed of vows, fears, and survival tactics—words that we have written on our own hearts with tears and dreams. The writing of this script began the first day of our lives and continues to this present moment. It is a concise expression of our deepest groanings. This script is our modus operandi; it governs our lives in ways we cannot fully understand.

A variety of topics are discussed within the script: how to survive emotional loss, how to handle deep disappointments, how to react when you feel you don't belong, etc. Under each of these headings, explicit instructions are offered to "remedy" the particular circumstance. When we are hard pressed and the pressure is on, our more superficial convictions give way to the deep patterns and entitlements of our written code of conduct.

Here is the good news: There is *another script*. This one resides deep in God's heart. It is His prophetic word for your life, a word that speaks of your identity and destiny in Christ. This script describes us more beautifully than we can imagine. The prophetic script is all about our potential—God's dream for us—a magnificent, breathtaking and inspiring vision for our lives.

Though you have rehearsed your life script for years and years, it need not be your destiny. Do not allow it to rule you any longer. In the name of Jesus, set your natural script before the cross and ask the Lord to place in your heart the prophetic script He has written for you. Exchange one declaration for the other. Allow the Great Physician to minister deep and tender healing in the areas of identity and destiny. The more you are released on the inside, the more able you will be to extend Spirit-filled, anointed ministry to others.

Detaching the Tethers

The script's influence in our lives can be likened to tethers that extend from our hearts and attach to people, ideas, and things. For some of us, the tethers have existed for such a long time that these attachments seem normal and right. But if the script is to be replaced, all of the ties that bind must be detached. This work is intensive; it doesn't happen overnight. But be encouraged: God is an excellent surgeon and He is able to set us free. He desires to release us into Spirit-filled ministry, but we must be willing to let go of these attachments and lay quietly on the operating table, entrusting ourselves fully to the One who called us into His service.

Some tethers that must be detached:

People's Opinions

With the Lord's help, detach the tether that causes you to cater to people's opinions. Replace the fear of people with the fear of the Lord. Fear that you might step away from your holy walk with Him. Fear that you are not rightly dividing the Word of God. But never fear or be intimidated by people. There are literally thousands of pastors who cater to the whims of others. There are only a few who are willing to speak the truth in love no matter what the cost. Choose this day to be a minister of the gospel who cannot be bought or intimidated.

In addition, be careful of the contracts you make with people. Some contracts are unconscious ones; we don't even know we're forging an agreement. Some examples:

> *"I will continue to hear your complaint as*
> *long as you remain in the church."*
> *"Because you do so much for the church, you*
> *are allowed to be crabby to people."*
> *"I will allow you to teach that Bible study,*
> *even though I know you are not fully*
> *reconciled to the elder team."*
> *"As long as you are loyal to me, I will be*
> *loyal to you."*

Such relational contracts will compromise your call and must be avoided at all costs. In the end, the only agreements a pastor should make in his/her ministry are to follow Jesus by the power of the Holy Spirit, to love each person with the love of Christ, and to speak the truth in love.

Money

Detach from being controlled by money in any way. Of course, you need to make a living. But will you be a slave to the paycheck? Pastors, which will influence us more: the offering box or the Word of God? Disconnect yourself from the idea that your ministry is a job. You are employed by the church leadership, but you are called by God. The congregation doesn't own you.

This is a key distinction that must be grounded in the very foundation of your heart. There will be times in your ministry when people with means will attempt to impose their influence on you. In subtle and not so subtle ways, they will let you know that if you don't agree with them, they will take their membership (and their tithe) and move to another church.[14]

Longstanding Alliances

Pastor, a person who is presently one of your strongest and healthiest allies may one day not even be a member of your church. Believe me, it doesn't take much for such a shift to happen. Detach from the expectation that this person or that person will never leave. Pray this: "Lord, I am thankful for the wonderful co-workers I have. Help me build healthy and true partnerships for Your Kingdom. But my loyalty is to You and to You alone. Though none go with me, still I will follow—no turning back, no turning back."

Criticism

In your ministry, you will discover marvelous and wondrous ways of disappointing people—by speaking too long (or not long enough), by being too structured (or too flexible), and by visiting too soon (or coming too late). Face this truth right now: You are not going to measure up in this or that person's book. Be more concerned about how you're measuring up in God's book!

Someone will not like what you wear, or what your spouse wears, or the way you worship, or the way you pray. Others will comment regularly on your preaching. *"You shouldn't share stories about yourself when you preach,"* or *"You should be more transparent and share stories about yourself when you preach."* The list goes on and on and on. Detach the tether that causes you to take criticism personally.

As trees and rocks are part of the forest terrain, so is criticism part of the ministry terrain. It is always going to be part of the scenery. Do your best. Preach the Word. Keep listening; keep growing and learning. You'll be fine. Just don't expect everyone to be in the cheering section.

Dedicating Time and Resources

Detach from the idea that your calling is to fix every problem that finds its way into your church. Some people are addicted to crisis. They want relief but are not willing to do the work required for transformative change. There are families I have worked with for years, dedicating hours and sometimes days to assist them, pray for them, care for them, go to bat for them, cry with them, stand with them. All the while, I was serving them as unto the Lord. I was counting on the thought that, *"If we can just get over this hurdle, the family will begin to thrive."*

In almost every situation where a family seemed to require an inordinate amount of effort and ministry time, all my giving seemed to have little or no effect. As a matter of fact, most of these families became resentful that *more* church resources weren't being allocated to their cause. Some families are takers. They are not bad people; they simply have no sense of boundaries and are blind to their sense of entitlement.

The church is not primarily a counseling center, a loan office, or a food bank. The church is a community of believers who gather to be equipped by the Word and the Spirit and are then sent into the world to advance the Kingdom of God. We can preach this truth every Sunday, but if we continue relating to people according to their entitlements, our words will be swept away by the tsunami waves of our co-dependent actions.

Moving Forward

Are there more tethers in ministry? Of course! Attachments involving loyalty, success and failure, appearance—these are really just a few. We can find ourselves inadvertently tethered to almost anything.

As our script tethers are detached, we begin to manifest our true calling as ambassadors of our Lord's message and lifestyle. We are called to extend the Kingdom of God wherever we go—in our homes, on the streets, in the lion's den, in our ministry meetings, in prayer meetings, in counseling sessions. He has called us to be His witnesses both locally and globally. What He has called us to do can be accomplished through the power of His Spirit.

Remember who you are. In Christ, you are an environment-changer. A fully surrendered believer carries tremendous authority in the spiritual realm. David's mighty men accomplished powerful feats for God's glory. Josheb-Basshebeth "raised his spear against eight hundred men, whom he killed in one encounter" (2Sam.23:8). Eleazar "stood his ground and struck down the Philistines till his hand grew tired and froze to the sword" (2Sam.23:9). Shammah "took his stand in the middle of the field and struck the Philistines down" (2Sam.23:12). Even greater power than what these mighty men experienced is available to you through the Spirit of God.

The Psalmist speaks of not fearing "the tens of thousands drawn up against me on every side" (Ps.3:6). You and I can stand against thousands in the Name of Jesus, but first, we must stand victoriously against the natural power of the mirror and the script.

Do the inner work. Tap into His power. Discover who you are in Christ and fulfill your destiny as a powerful warrior of the Most High God!

The weapons we fight with are not the weapons of
the world. On the contrary, they have divine power
to demolish strongholds. We demolish arguments
and every pretension that sets itself up against
the knowledge of God, and we take captive every
thought to make it obedient to Christ.
2 Corinthians 10:4-5

Survival Key #3
Know Your Enemy

There are two equal and opposite errors into which our race can fall about the devils. One is to disbelieve in their existence. The other is to believe, and to feel an excessive and unhealthy interest in them. They themselves are equally pleased by both errors, and hail a materialist or a magician with the same delight.
    —C.S. Lewis[15]

On the road that leads from 'walking in the flesh' to 'walking in the spirit,' the evil one brings his strongest opposition. He works to keep you earthbound and weak. And you may well imagine that he wants no soul to find its way on this path of life, where you no longer rely on your own understanding. Therefore, he wants to turn you back from this way of true ascendancy and strength in God alone.
    —John of the Cross[16]

Therefore put on the full armor of God, so that when the day of evil comes, you may be able to stand your ground, and after you have done everything, to stand.

— Ephesians 6:13

Who is your enemy? It is not the person who slanders you or the group of congregants who apply political pressure to sway a church decision. It is not the person who is persecuting you or the neighbors who wish for your demise. The enemy we struggle against is not "flesh and blood" (Eph.6:12); he is spiritual and more evil than we can imagine. Satan, the devil, "prowls around like a roaring lion looking for someone to devour" (1Pe.5:8). He hates the name of Jesus and labors to veil the glory of Christ by "blinding the minds of unbelievers so that they cannot see the light of the gospel" (2Cor.4:4).

> *The adversary (along with his army of fallen angels) never gets tired, does not fight fairly and is set upon your destruction.*

Why is he attacking you? You are a child of God. If someone really wants to hurt me, that person will attack my children. Satan desires to take as many people to hell with him as he can. Every child of the King that he captures and kills brings pain to the very heart of our heavenly Father.

In his famous work, *The Art of War*, Sun Tsu writes: "One who knows the enemy and knows himself will not be in danger in a hundred battles. One who does not know the enemy but knows himself will sometimes win, sometimes lose. One who does not know the enemy and does not know himself will be in danger in every battle." No competent commanding officer would lead his or her troops into battle without first attaining proper intelligence concerning

51

the assets and vulnerabilities of the opposing army. In like manner, you must become cognizant of the cunning strategies of your adversary in order to survive in ministry.

Some of these strategies—such as weariness, discouragement and isolation—are so subtle that you may assume there is no supernatural component involved at all. I have come to believe that the enemy will use *any* circumstance to his advantage and our destruction (even circumstances that he did not create).

Therefore, do not be casual concerning this battlefield: Spiritual warfare is an on-going, daily reality for every pastor. Your adversary (along with his army of fallen angels) never gets tired, does not fight fairly, and is set upon your destruction. Keep your eyes on our Commander-in-Chief, but also be aware of the following strategies of your adversary.

Attrition and Weariness

I have discovered that much of the enemy's plan to destroy us has to do with wearing us down and wearing us out. Satan believes he can outlast us. He believes that eventually we will give up. Be aware of this strategy. Take time to rest!

Realize that the terrain changes quickly in ministry. One week, it feels like the world is falling in on you; it feels like things couldn't get worse. Don't react, attack, or retreat. Just stand! Stand in faith. These moments of difficulty will pass in due time. It is important that you see that God is able to sustain you in the midst of trials.

The next week everything seems to be going well. Be thankful, but realize there will be challenging days ahead. Don't give yourself to opinions, emotions, or circumstances. Move in the Spirit. Stay on the trail. Keep running the race.

Pastoring is not a sprint; it is a marathon.

Did you have a tough day? Get some space. Take a nap. Go see a movie. Take a walk. Listen to some music. Don't overreact to the day. Rather, respond by the Spirit. Instead of reacting to the daily fluctuations of the "spiritual stock exchange," choose to be a long-term investor in the Word of God. If you remain faithful, your ministry will reap eternal dividends.

The enemy loves to place a large map of the Sahara Desert in front of your face and remind you how difficult your journey is going to be. As you look at the many challenges set before you, a demon whispers in your ear, "Even if you make it through this day, look how far you still have to go. It going to take you weeks, months, even decades to get across this desert and you are thirsty already. Give up now! Turn around! Go back to Egypt!" Discouragement is a powerful weapon. The enemy wants you to become overwhelmed and to give up the ground you've worked so hard to gain.

Refuse to look at the enemy's maps. Reject the lies that you just can't make it, and that you are in a battle you just can't win. Remember the Lord's words: "Do not worry about tomorrow. . .each day has enough trouble of its own" (Mt.6:34). When you are weary, don't think too much or talk too much. Don't even glance at the big map when you're tired. Set your sites on getting to the next shelter where you can rest.

By the way, this is the good news that your adversary conveniently forgets to share: There is a shelter waiting for you. There is a place of safety, a strong tower, a place of refreshment and repair. God Himself longs to be your oasis in the desert. In times of weariness, He is more than able to minister to you and give you living water to drink.

Look around you. Thousands of pastors are suffering under the desert sun. They found themselves unexpectedly in this unforgiving environment and did not know how to find the Oasis. You, however, must become accustomed to the wilderness regions. You must learn how to wait out the mid-day sun. In the desert, a camel is preferable to the finest thoroughbred horse. Learn from the camel; discover how to survive in the hot sand and the burning heat.

Thank God in the midst of your weariness, for there are lessons that can only be learned in the wilderness. It is there that you discover how God tenderly ministers and gives you victory in this battle of attrition. In these seasons, you learn about thirst and the power of living water.

Distancing

Another of Satan's great strategies is to interrupt your intimacy with God and create distance between you and your Lord. He knows that every step you take away from Christ makes you more vulnerable for attack. If you move away from dependency upon Jesus just an inch or two every day, you may lose sight of Him altogether in a couple of weeks.

When you were walking right beside the Lord, you felt His breath upon your neck and sensed His gentle promptings throughout the day. From a distance, His voice isn't as clear. You've begun to trust your own understanding and view things from your own perspective. Inch by inch, the enemy has lured you away. Instead of your relationship with the Lord being the priority of your heart, other things— ministry, people, and responsibilities— now occupy the center. The sanctuary of your heart has become a marketplace of busyness. The shift is subtle, but don't be fooled. Luring you away from God is a potent strategy of the enemy. From the outside it seems as if your life hasn't changed, but inside your heart has grown cold and your faith stale. This is a frightening spiritual condition. You arrive at that place by moving away from Christ just a little every day.

When you are walking by the Spirit, the enemy has no hope for victory. But separation from God provides the enemy with the leverage he needs to destroy you. Don't give him an inch. Stay close with your Lord.

The enemy wants you to be anywhere except right beside the Lord. He is fine with you lagging behind Jesus. He is equally satisfied if you run ahead. So keep your eyes on your Lord; don't venture out on your own.

Isolation

Do you have people praying for you? Do you have people in your life who know you? Just as a pack of wild dogs look for the isolated wildebeest, demons are searching for pastors who have separated themselves from their co-workers and support structures. When you are isolated and running on your own, you are vulnerable. Believe me, the wild dogs are watching you all the time and waiting for just the right time to attack. Pull back from the front lines when you need to rest, but don't pull away from your accountability, your prayer coverage, and fellowship with your closest warriors. Don't venture out in the field alone; the enemy will be on you in no time.

> *A fiery dart attacks a person's identity and destiny. When you are pierced in this way, seek the Lord to discover what lies have been introduced into your heart.*

The Fiery Dart

A fiery dart is a demonically charged weapon strategically aimed at a vulnerable domain of your life and ministry. If it is not blocked by your shield of faith, it can do great damage. Such an attack can come at any time and at any place: at a party, at a prayer meeting, among friends, in the middle of a worship service, in the middle of the most docile conversation. The symptoms vary. It may become difficult for you to think clearly or even to articulate what you are feeling, but you sense that something has invaded you deeply, to the very core of your being.

A fiery dart attacks a person's identity and destiny. It is often coated with lies about one's personal worth and value. When you have been pierced in this way, seek the Lord to discover what lies have been introduced into your heart. Confess, repent, and take back the ground in the Name of Christ. Declare the promises of God that directly refute those lies. Remove the dart and ask your close confidants to pray over you for healing.

The All-Out Assault

In addition to the more subtle, cunning, individual threats mentioned above, there will be times when the enemy attacks you from every side. You will be overwhelmed and will experience feelings of resignation, hopelessness, and fear. Often, these brutal attacks take place immediately after spiritual victories.

I cannot describe how important it is for you to reach out for your Father's hand when these attacks come upon you. When you are under a full assault, your only shelter is to hide in the "cleft of the rock." Only here will you find power to stand even in the hurricane, as you simply cling to Jesus.

These all-out assaults last for a time, but they *will* pass. Remember this when they come. Every warrior-pastor must learn to walk through these vicious storms. No matter what you feel in the moment, if you cling to Jesus, you will emerge victorious.

Moving Forward

Casual mindsets about the strategies and traps of the enemy have led many pastors to the brink of destruction. Remember this: Every hour of every day, the adversary is seeking to destroy you. His strategic attacks may come at anytime and anywhere—in your thoughts and feelings, in your relationships, in your home, in your office—throughout your life and ministry.

Therefore, work to become competent in the domain of spiritual warfare. Study and find yourself approved in this strategic area of ministry.[17] The key to victory resides in the principles of confession, repentance, and complete surrender to Jesus. Remember who lives inside of you. The enemy is powerful, but the Holy Spirit is exponentially greater. Satan has no ground to defeat us except through our ignorance, fear, and disobedience. Walk in the authority that was purchased for every believer through the cross of Christ, and, with a mature eye and a fearless heart, take your place on the battlefield to fight for the release of captives in the name of Jesus!

Praise be to the Lord, Who has not let us be torn
by their teeth. We have escaped like a bird from
the fowler's snare; the snare has been broken,
and we have escaped.
Psalm 124:6-7

Survival Key #4
Know the Terrain

It's better to have empty pews (in our case, chairs) than seats filled with antagonists. Empty pews usually leave the church's vision intact. But the wrong kind of people tamper with our values and exert a negative influence on the church. New churches seem especially vulnerable to antagonists, who are frequently looking for new power bases. They are black holes of spiritual energy, sucking out the resolve of those around them.

—Paul Johnson, journalist and historian[18]

In a free country, to be a member of a church, it is enough to believe and to be baptized. In the Church underground it is not enough to be a member in it. You can be baptized and you can believe, but you will not be a member of the Underground Church unless you know how to suffer. You might have the mightiest faith in the world, but if you are not prepared to suffer, then you will be taken by the police. You will get two slaps and you will declare anything. So the preparation for suffering is one of the essentials of the preparation of underground work.

— Richard Wurmbrand, founder of Voice of
  the Martyrs[19]

There was a time in my life when I went through intense trials such as I had never faced before. I became rude and harsh with those closest to me. My family and friends began to avoid me. I cried out to the Lord, 'Where is all this anger coming from? It wasn't here before!'

The Lord responded, *'Son, it is when they liquefy gold in fire that the impurities show up.'* He then asked a question that changed my life. *'Can you see the impurities in gold before it is put in the fire?'*

'No,' I answered.

'But that doesn't mean they were not there,' He said. *'When the fire of trials hit you, these impurities surfaced. Though hidden to you, they were always visible to Me. So now you have a choice that will determine your future. You can remain angry, blaming your wife, friends, pastor, and the people you work with, or you can see this dross of sin for what it is and repent, receive forgiveness, and I will take My ladle and remove these impurities from your life.'*

— John Bevere, evangelist and Bible teacher[20]

The terrain of ministry is full of life-giving opportunities. It is also full of snares. Become a student of the battlefield upon which your ministry will either rise or fall. You must have open and seeing eyes. Take notice of both the high places that offer advantage and the valleys that make you vulnerable. Decide now to become a student of the terrain. Be alert and aware; your life depends on it.

The Holy Spirit desires for us to be "wise as serpents and innocent as doves" (Mt.10:16). Our enemy is setting traps and snares throughout the battlefield in order to destroy us. We must train ourselves to see what others don't normally see. What looks safe at first glance may not be safe. A good trap is hidden from sight. A good snare entices its prey with attractive bait. We cannot afford to be fooled.

A good trap is hidden from sight. A good snare entices its prey with attractive bait. We cannot afford to be fooled.

Pits

Watch your step; watch your heart! There are deep pits all around you. These cavernous and cold places have names like "anger," "resentment," and "bitterness." They exist throughout the terrain of ministry and pose a very real danger.

Understand that you *will* encounter mistreatment and various forms of persecution as you minister in the name of

Christ. Such attacks — and remember that we battle not against flesh and blood — will strike at the very core of your personhood and identity. There will be times when you are misrepresented and slandered by brothers and sisters whom you've walked with for years. Others will believe lies about you and leave the church. At times, you will become angry and full of pain. Don't strike back. Realize that your emotions will blind you from seeing clearly. Before you know it, you can be swallowed up in those deep pits.

Survival Tactic:

If you have fallen into one of these pits, there are ways to escape and recover. God can provide spiritual ropes and ladders through His grace and through the community of faith. However, as with all weaknesses and snares, it is far better to avoid them altogether.

To do this, you must learn how not to allow your emotional pain governance over your actions. Max Lucado refers to this danger when he writes, "Linger too long in the stench of your hurt, and you'll smell like the toxin you despise."[22] Many pastors have fallen into a pit of anger and resentment, and some never recover. To avoid this, I encourage you to have the conversations that are necessary and then to extend forgiveness and release people. Christian author and poet George Herbert articulated it well when he said, "He who cannot forgive another, breaks the bridge over which he must pass himself."

Carnal Temptations

As fourth-century philosopher Mencius said, "Before a man can do things there must be things he will not do." No one is exempt from having to battle the time-tested carnal temptations of the flesh and the world.

Do not underestimate the power of lust. Every pastor knows that "the cravings of sinful man, the lust of his eyes and the boasting of what he has and does comes not from the Father but from the world" (1Jn.2:16). Nonetheless, many thousands have fallen into the miry clay of pornography, fantasy, and lewdness of all kinds. It is important to note that lust includes a craving for illicit intimacy — an emotional affair and/or deep companionship with a person that crosses healthy boundaries. In these cases, we are being lured into satisfying our God-given desires (to be loved, to be known, to be affirmed, to be comforted, etc.) in an ungodly way.

The world unashamedly promotes sensuality: on the internet, on the streets, on television. It is so accessible and attractive to the carnal nature, but hidden beneath the bait is a deadly hook. Satan is a fisherman of souls, and lust is one of his shiniest lures.

> *Satan is a fisherman of souls and lust is one of his shiniest lures.*

The Survival Tactic:

Establish accountability with two or three pastors (of your own gender and not in your church) concerning your thought life and struggles with any unholy patterns. Meet consistently with this group and pray for one another.

Be on alert at all times, but especially when you are under stress. It is in those moments that you will crave comfort and immediate satisfaction. Your enemy will place a shiny lure right before your eyes when you are most hungry for a hug.

In addition, strengthen your ability for self-control by abstaining from different things. Abstain from sugar, television, or (forbid the thought) even coffee for a time—if only to exercise your ability to combat the craving for comfort. Learn to say "no" to immediate gratification. Apply the Apostle Paul's testimony to yourself: "I beat my body and make it my slave, so that after I have preached to others, I myself will not be disqualified for the prize" (1 Cor.9:27).

In these moments you must choose Jesus over sin. If you train for the battle daily, you will be able to hold out and hold on when temptation comes knocking. It is true: You can be victorious only in *His* strength. However, you must use *your* willpower to choose His strength. Develop the muscles of your will by practicing the discipline of saying "no" to yourself.

Keep watch. Someone is fishing for your soul every minute of every day and every night. There is a hook, a terrible hook, hidden in the bait.

Stress-filled Moments and Settings

Most pastors are able to extend grace and offer kindness to others when life is going well, but how do you relate when life becomes stressful? How do you respond to people when you are hungry or tired? Ministry is full of surprises. Sudden changes and unanticipated challenges will meet you almost every day. I've seen talented pastors discredit themselves in a few short, pressurized moments by their reaction to a stressful time. It wasn't just the moment that destroyed them, but the lack of preparation leading up to it. People are watching! Your demeanor in the midst of trials will make or break your testimony.

The Survival Tactic:
Learn how to feed off stress-filled circumstances instead of those circumstances feeding off of you! When the whole room is filled with anxiety, be the one who is able to remain peaceful. When the whole team loses hope, be the one who reclaims it. When others lash out, be the one who does not react out of the flesh. When others resign, be the one who continues to stand.

In order to walk by the Spirit when circumstances become challenging, you must have eyes to see what is happening in the spiritual realm. Observe and learn. Recognize that the Lord has brought you to this stress-filled environment for a reason. He's giving you an opportunity to shine for Him! Don't allow your surroundings to control you. Remember who you are and whose blood runs through your veins. You have but one Master: the Lord Jesus! Therefore, do not bow your knee to circumstances or be conformed to the moment. Choose to walk in the power of God and be an instrument of His peace, grace and love.

> *In stressful moments, in the crucible of the flame, the talking kind of faith becomes exposed and the standing kind of faith is revealed.*

People need to see something more than the talking kind of faith in their pastor. Everyone performs well on calm and sunny days. A person's true colors become apparent when the storms hit. In stressful moments, in the crucible of the flame, the talking kind of faith becomes exposed and the standing kind of faith is revealed.

Do you want the standing kind of faith? If so, you must observe what happens to your body, mind and spirit when you encounter stress. Learn how you naturally respond when you're hungry, when you're offended, when you're tired. Discover your natural limits and then begin to stretch those limits.

Like a professional athlete who learns to perform competently even when injured, so each of us must learn to practice self-control in the midst of difficult circumstances. Go to the edge on your own. Fast for a day and pray all night, and then attend your elder meeting. Observe yourself. Learn how irritability, distraction and offense are magnified when your body isn't fully content.

Keep alert. Stress can enter into your life anywhere and at anytime. Be careful to keep your head when you're tired, hungry and frustrated. Be aware of stressful moments and seize those opportunities to be an environment-changer.

Sabotage: Turning You against You

There are sounds—echoes of the past—that have the ability to cause us to cringe in the present. These are emotional echoes or associations that control us.[21]

A river of pain flows through your life. It flows with the tears, hurts, and disappointments you've experienced during your years on earth. Whenever you experience fresh pain, the water level and the speed of the current of this river grow.

Satan is a terrorist, and he has plans to make use of your river of pain. His hope is that you will ignore it until it overflows its banks and wreaks havoc in your life and ministry. You must be proactive in dealing with this river of pain before it destroys you. Allow all your injuries, all your disappointments, all your hurts, all your pain and shame to flow to the foot of the cross. If you don't, one day this toxic river will flood your relationships and devastate your ministry.

The same is true of other aspects of your fleshly nature. Are you thirsty for affirmation and approval? The enemy will capitalize on that need. Are you lonely and starving for intimacy? The enemy will introduce an inappropriate avenue of satisfaction. Are you susceptible to pride? Don't be surprised if you are offered a kingdom. Are you insecure? Be sure that the enemy will try to shame you. Satan will discover any attitude in you that resonates with the spirit of carnality, and he will call it to allegiance.

The Survival Tactic:

Recognize that you may be able to hide your vulnerabilities from the people around you, but any sinful attitude or behavior is a giant bull's eye in the spiritual realm. Neutralize all of these by way of confession and pleading the blood of Christ. After that, be sure to put on the belt of truth, because arguments that set themselves up against the knowledge of God (2Cor.10:5) will assuredly be coming your way.

Comparison

Comparing ourselves or our churches to others is a common and tenacious trap. It is common in that the enemy sets this trap frequently and in many domains of ministry. It is tenacious because once we fall prey to its claws, escape is difficult.

Comparison traps succeed when our eyes shift from a singular focus on Jesus to a roaming focus on other people and other things. The very minute our audience becomes more than One, the vicious claw of this trap is already being sprung.

People will push you into this comparison trap (usually unintentionally):

> *"My previous pastor was somebody who just*
> *loved people."*
> *"I just love it when your associate pastor*
> *preaches—he's my favorite."*
> *"The new charismatic church down the street*
> *is growing by one hundred people a week!*
> *Wow—God is really moving in that place.*
> *Why aren't we growing like that?"*

The Survival Tactic:

Jesus has called you to shepherd your flock faithfully. Keep your eye on this task. Be thankful for the other generals in the field who are waging war to save souls. If they are commanding a larger regiment, so be it. The Great General sees the whole battlefield and is watching how you train and lead your soldiers. Take your cues from Him and Him alone.

Get this straight in your heart and fix your eyes upon Jesus. There will always be someone who smarter, quicker, wittier, more gifted than you. There will always be pastors who are better administrators or who seem to have more energy than you. Stop the madness that comes from comparing. Be yourself. Do not evaluate your success by looking at others. Be faithful in your call and rejoice that you are working with others all around the world for the cause of Christ!

Sleeping Potion

Something as obvious as swallowing a sleeping potion may seem like a small risk, but have you ever succumbed to the thought, *"I'll just rest my eyes here for a few minutes..."*? Before you know it, years have passed by and nothing has changed. "A little sleep, a little slumber, a little folding of the hands to rest—and poverty will come on you like a bandit and scarcity like an armed man" (Prov.6:10-11).

The Survival Tactic:
Do not fall asleep on the battlefield! Keep awake and alert! When you move in the power of the Holy Spirit, there will be an edge to your life. Keep the edge. Don't become casual. Rest only in safe places and when you know someone else is keeping watch on the wall.

Toxins

Complaining and Spirit-quenching are like toxins in the Body of Christ. They will prevent growth. There are people in every church who have become quite accomplished in the art of complaining. Their eyes move to and fro throughout the sanctuary. They see everything and talk about it too. They complain about everything under the sun: what this person wears, how that person repeats himself, how she prays too long, how he's too loud in worship. This group can steal away every ounce of joy within a worship service, but only if you let them.

Complainers are relentless. They have lost the ability to be content in all situations and thankful in everything. These are sins that have somehow become permissible within the church, even though

> *Once the free flow of toxins has ceased, the air will begin to clear in your corporate services. A new freedom will begin to emerge.*

they are terribly destructive. They quench, sour, and choke the growth of your congregation. If you allow it, this negativity will also take its toll on you, filling you with discouragement and hopelessness.

Other spiritual toxins include discouragement, fear, depression, gossip, slander, and anxiety. Some poisons (like discouragement and depression) might require prolonged exposure or repeated ingestion to shut down a ministry. Some (like fear, gossip, and slander) are potent, quickly attacking the neurological system of the church, causing paralysis or even death.

The Survival Tactic:

Work with your elders to create a "fresh air" environment where young plants can flourish. Imagine planting a garden and then allowing someone to spray poison on your plants. Sour faces, sour glances, and sour words are like poison in a church. I'm not speaking about the attitudes and actions of visitors entering into the doors of your church. Anyone who's spent any time within a church community knows that the complainers are usually longstanding members who have lost their first love and who resent anyone who still has some measure of passion and faith.

Eradicate complaining, gossip, and judgment within your church. Stand against these sins that kill "first love" worship and "first love" life! Stand guard at the gate of your garden. Teach your people that complaining is not Christ-like behavior and that extending grace is!

Imagine laughing at a five-year old trying to learn how to read; she might get discouraged and give up on learning. In the same way, it is wrong to complain when a believer doesn't get everything perfect when sharing her testimony or when offering a prophetic word. Someone complaining about this might shut down a wonderful prophetic gift in the Body of Christ. There is a place for loving correction; there is no place for complaining or hurtful criticism. Create an environment of learning and acceptance wherein people will be encouraged to step out of the boat and try walking on water.

The church must see your vigilance in this regard. Correct mishaps and immature behavior. The congregation must see that sloppy ministry is not our best testimony to the world. Correct laziness, and press your congregation toward excellence, but save your rebukes for the complainer. Pastor, I admonish you to set the stake concerning complaining and gossip. Permit it no longer! As your church begins to clean out the toxins, you will discover that you've made some enemies in the camp. Complainers are prideful people. Do not be surprised if some people decide to leave your church if they can't "be themselves" and "give their opinion about everything." In spite of this, don't give an inch on this battlefield. The negativity must die in the name of Jesus.

Once the free flow of toxins has ceased, the air will begin to clear in your corporate services. A new freedom, a new gentleness, a new excitement will begin to emerge. What has happened in the spiritual realm? People who once were afraid to find their voice and share their gifts are now stepping forward. The Holy Spirit has now been given room to minister through His church. This is the whole point of corporate services: to recognize the King of glory and humbly follow His lead. Such an environment is incredibly sweet! It may have been birthed at great cost, but it is priceless and cannot be forfeited.

The antidotes for all spiritual toxins are the blood of the Lamb, obedience to the Word of God, and the choice to walk by faith not by sight. Be prepared for chemical attacks and keep the air in your church fresh and holy.

The Minefield of Relationships

Perhaps the phrase "minefield of relationships" seems pessimistic, an exaggeration of the danger. But I believe that this realm is the most treacherous terrain that you will face in your career. There is a tendency for pastors to look outside the camp for attacks, but friendly fire is a real and present danger in every ministry context.

God desires pastors to establish and enjoy healthy relationships. And what God desires for us can be accomplished. But relationships are complex and the minefield we must cross has real explosives.

The Survival Tactic:

A minefield can be crossed with proper equipment. It is a matter of knowing where the explosives are. The One who clears the path of danger will show you precisely where to place your feet. Jesus will guide you on this journey. Let me give you some examples of the explosives in the field of relationships.

Loyalty

Fallacy: *"If you love me and respect me, you will have my back no matter what the circumstance. You will keep my secrets, even if the secrets are not healthy ones."*

Be loyal to people for the sake of the Kingdom, not for the sake of the relationship. Reverence communication, but do not be a secret-keeper. Healthy relationships welcome truth-speaking and honesty. Healthy relationships are not co-dependent and hidden. Keep a sharp eye out for loyalty issues. They are often invisible (unconscious and unseen in the relationship) but very strong.

Ledger

Fallacies: *"You owe me. I took care of you in the past—and now I'm calling in a favor."*
"You made a mistake and I forgave you. But it was a bad mistake and you are still indebted to me."

Healthy relationships have a balanced ledger; one party doesn't "owe" the other party an extraordinary amount of emotional currency. Keep your accounts clean. If you are indebted to someone, work hard to pay back the debt in a healthy way. Do not be blackmailed or manipulated by the ledger. If you can be manipulated or bought, you have lost your moral authority.

Transparency

Fallacy: *"Pastor, I shared some of my deepest sins and struggles with you. Now it's your turn."*

Mutuality is a very positive characteristic of healthy friendships, but most often in counseling and in your ministry as a pastor, personal transparency is a misstep and a relational snare. Your congregation needs to see you sharing about yourself *appropriately*. They need to know that you do share more deeply in some type of accountability/support group, but you have no obligation to share yourself with them. They need rather to see you communicating with healthy boundaries.

Pastor as Friend

Fallacy: *"Now that we are friends, you look different to me when you're preaching."*

God desires for you to have healthy relationships within your congregation, but be careful with whom you expose your deeper thoughts, feelings, and journey. Be careful with whom you relax. Everyone knows that you're not perfect, but some will struggle when they see your imperfections or even when they witness your humanness as you get tired or silly, or when you daydream about other ministry settings, etc.

True friendship takes time to develop. Do not reveal "level 8" feelings in the first months of the relationship, even if you sense a deep trustworthiness within the person. Start with a "level 4 or 5." In time, the relationship may develop further, but err on the side of caution.

Even then, among your friends, do not abdicate your authority as pastor. A good friend will value and respect your position and will be able to separate friendship conversations from pastoral ones. This takes maturity. Have many good, open, and real relationships within the church, but keep an eye on boundaries. You are called to be the pastor, not the friend, of the flock God has given you.

Moving Forward

Avoid the dangers I have mentioned above, but also be proactive by looking to the terrain-changing machinery of prayer, worship, preaching, and equipping (detailed in Survival key #6) in order to create acres and acres of fruit-producing saints for the Kingdom of God.

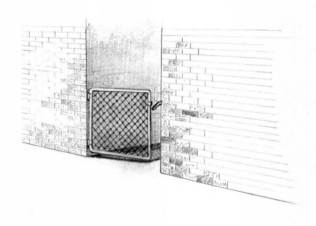

But Jesus would not entrust himself to them, for he knew all people. He did not need human testimony about them, for he knew what was in them.
John 2:24-25

Survival key #5
Know Your Boundaries

Like most pastors, I enjoy being accessible. It makes me feel useful, almost indispensable. And after years of experience, I'm pretty good at overseeing the operation of the church. But there is a downside. Always being available drains me. When I'm drained, I lose perspective. I begin to think God's kingdom is our local church, and our church is one problem after another! The vision is hard to come by. Also, the more I'm available to people, curiously enough, the less they seem to respect me, mainly because I'm not taking care of a crucial element of my calling. Years ago a man said to me: "Why are you always here when I call? Haven't you got anything more important to do than hang around the office? If we had wanted a crisis manager, we would have hired a fireman!"

—Joel C. Hunter, senior pastor of Northland Church in Longwood, FL[22]

I had a difficult conversation several years ago with a friend in the ministry who had fallen because of adultery. I asked, "What in the world were you doing? Didn't you hear the alarm bells going off?"

There was a long silence, then the man answered, "Oh Bob, I did hear the alarms. I heard the alarms plainly. But when I heard the alarms I decided to disconnect the wires."

—Dr. Bob Reccord, speaker and author[23]

In His earthly ministry, Jesus never turned anyone away. At the same time, He did not allow everyone to have complete access to Him. He disclosed Himself most fully to His Father. Then, at differing levels, He disclosed His heart to the three, the twelve, the seventy and the multitudes.

We are not called to be independent or co-dependent, but inter-dependent with other believers. We are called to community, but what does this mean? How closely are we to travel together?

Your survival will depend in part on how you answer these questions and, more specifically, on your ability to establish and respect healthy boundaries. Boundaries are walls, fences, doors and gates — not simply in the physical realm, but in the emotional, relational, and spiritual realms as well.

Consider the doors of your home. Are they propped open at all hours of the day or do you close and even lock them at various times? Can just anyone enter your house at any time of the day or night? Of course not! In the same way, you must stand watch and attend to your emotional/spiritual doors, especially in the following domains.

Boundaries of Time and Schedule

Nearly every church member says, "Pastor, we want you to get away—be with your family, take time for yourself." At the same time, the following expectation hangs over the altar of the church like a masterpiece in an art museum: "Pastor, you will be available whenever I need you."

Yes, there is much talk in church about "family first" and "taking care of yourself," but in reality the congregation expects you to be on call 24 hours a day, 7 days a week, 365 days a year until you die (and let's hope that doesn't come at an inconvenient time). That agreement lives not only in other people's expectations, but perhaps in your heart as well.

Many pastors have unconsciously agreed to try to meet these unrealistic expectations. I was one of them. I can tell you from experience that you will fail, even when you try your very best and your heart is in the right place. You will visit the hospital room eight days in a row but when you miss the ninth day—you suddenly become *the pastor who doesn't care*.

Stare at that masterpiece over the altar: "You will be available whenever I need you." Deal with this ancient inscription right from the beginning of your ministry. Is this the call of the pastor? I might be mistaken, but it sounds a lot like the Scripture, "I will never leave or forsake you" (He.13:5). It might be a good idea to discover who makes that claim (hint: the Uncreated One who is perfect in strength and wisdom and never sleeps). In order to fulfill such a call, a pastor will need Messianic credentials and a white horse. My white horse is old. My Messianic credentials are laughable. How about you?

It is a privilege to serve as a pastor, but realize that the work will never be completed. The needs and wants and opinions of church members will cry out to you continuously. You must learn, in responsible and appropriate ways, to step back from hurting people, unresolved conflicts, and decisions that have not been finalized. Learn to step away and to re-emerge. Your survival depends on acquiring these tools.

What if it really is a crisis? What if there is a suicide, or terminal cancer, or a particular family has no place to stay? First, remember that God is still on the throne. He is not surprised by the events of this day, and nothing is too difficult for Him. Take a deep breath. You are called to do your part, not God's part.

> *Do you have "I'm available all the time" engraved on your forehead? If so, kneel at the altar and deal once and for all with that ancient inscription.*

Second, unless it is simply impossible, *show up*. The ministry of presence is incredibly powerful. Linger. You don't need to have all the right answers. In fact, words are extremely over-rated in our line of work. Just show up and be present with your friends in their time of need. Third, *get others involved immediately.* God came up with the idea of community. Community is more than one person. You must be present, but one of your most important pastoral tasks is to help establish support systems around the persons and families among whom you minister.

Look in the mirror. Do you have the "I'm available all the time" sign engraved on your forehead? If so, kneel at the altar with your elder team and deal once and for all with that ancient inscription. Break the yoke that you will never be able to carry in the name of Christ. Serve the people in the power and wisdom and promptings of the Spirit of God, but have *no* other contract and listen to *no* other voice.

Guard Your Family

We've all heard the nightmare story about the pastor whom everyone loves. "*He's always there for us and the whole church. So caring, so wise, so gentle and kind! What a man of God!*" But his wife is bitter towards him. She feels abandoned. He's always on call. Even when he's home he's not really home. His children have rejected the church. This pastor has had an affair with his work, and the family hates him for it.

Learn from the thousands of shipwrecked pastors who have gone before you. If you are married, create a rigid boundary around family times. Your family relationships comprise a significant part of your calling on this earth. Your spouse and children need to be with you and you need to be with them. Chart the flow of your week, your spouse's week, and your children's week, and then choose to be present with you family at agreed upon times. Time at home is not simply time out of the office. You must be present. Turn the cell phone off; don't look at your e-mails. As much as is in your power, don't let your mind wander to the issues of the church. (Rest assured that they will be waiting for you tomorrow in all their glory).

The main point is this: Church ministry can easily consume every moment of your time and every ounce of your energy. If you don't set boundaries, you won't have a healthy marriage, a healthy family, or any real friendships. If this happens, you are in great danger of becoming a very strange and unlovely animal: the non-human, functional minister on his or her way to burning out. I can tell you with certainty that this is not God's design for any pastor. Therefore, create boundaries for your personal times with the Lord, for your times of study, for building intimacy with your spouse, for parenting your children, for your rest and recreation, for times together as a family, and for friends.

> *The main point is this: church ministry can easily take every ounce of your time. If you don't set boundaries, you won't have a healthy marriage, a healthy family or any real friendships.*

God created us to live a balanced life. The Hebrew word *shalom* not only connotes peace and welfare, but also right alignment and balance. The Christian walk can be likened to a balance beam. Speed and strength are admirable traits, but on the beam, balance is the key. Satan does not care what it is that throws us off balance; he simply wants us to fall. A Pastor who does not guard personal time and family time will lose balance and fall.

Emotional Boundaries

Whom do you bring into your inner sanctuary? To whom do you disclose your deeper self, both personally and professionally? Be careful, very careful, whom you trust. Gather people of character and maturity around you. Walk with individuals for at least three years before bringing them into your deeper counsel. No one is perfect; people will let you down.

Gender

Survey statistics from *Men's Secret Wars* indicate that sixty-four percent of pastors or church staff struggle with sexual addiction or compulsion.[24] Twenty-five percent admitted to having sexual intercourse with someone besides their wife while married, even after they had accepted Christ. Another fourteen percent admitted some form of sexual contact short of intercourse.

How do you steer clear of being one of these statistics? Begin simply. Men, don't meet alone with women. Women, don't meet alone with men. Create safe structures wherein no one has any ground to accuse you of impropriety. Establish safe and credible accountability when meeting people of the opposite gender so that you do not bring dishonor to your Lord and compromise your ministry career.

In addition, respect the power of physical touch. Some hugs can be good, some can be bad. The power of emotional touch is more subtle, but equally, if not more, powerful. Prayer, counseling, and spiritual discussions can be very intimate, and before you know it, an attraction can emerge. Many pastors who have fallen into sexual affairs can honestly say they had no plans or interest in the physical aspect of the relationship. Their emotional intimacy tank was empty. They were looking for companionship, a caring listener, a trusted confidant. Intimacy, the sharing of dreams and feelings, is a serious drug to the body and to the soul.

It is lovely when someone really listens, when someone truly cares. Emotional connection is like a direct injection of adrenalin into the human heart! Do not underestimate its power. People will come into your office depleted of hope and raw with feelings of abandonment and rejection. Your careful listening and authentic concern will seem to them like an oasis in the Sahara. Men, she is so thirsty for your kindness. It is something she just doesn't get from her husband. Women, he is craving the gentle support you are offering. His marriage is cold and he feels alone. Be very careful! Remember: God created us for intimacy. Be aware of your thirst for intimacy and how that thirst is met.

Our culture is obsessed with sex, and people are hungry for love. This is a dangerous combination. Anyone can be tempted and fall into sin. Pastors who believe they are immune to physical or emotional affairs are self-deceived and are leaving themselves wide open to attack.

If two people don't meet privately, it is difficult for a romantic attraction to develop, but don't be fooled. Phone calls, e-mails, and working in ministry together can also create a strong emotional connection. Before you know it, you find yourself "falling in love." In just a few short months you become involved in a relationship that could decimate your ministry call.

Relationally Wounded People

God calls you to love people as He loves them. Be wise as serpents and innocent as doves concerning this high and worthy call on your life. Realize that nearly every person has been wounded deeply in the realm of relationship, particularly in the foundational domain of trust. The giants of abandonment and rejection loom large on the horizon of our lives.

People bring their brokenness into the church. When they do, they are like a 5-year old boy walking around the house with his father's loaded gun. He doesn't understand the danger in his hand. He doesn't have bad intention. He is simply walking around the house with something he found in his father's closet.

Wounded people will walk into your office and into your church with loaded emotional guns. They do not know the extent of the danger that is in their hands. Beware! Even though most people do not have it in their minds to harm you, take care to protect yourself and others from people with emotional and relational weapons.

Highly Dangerous People

A final word of warning: At some point in your career, a person or persons within your church will attempt to destroy you and your ministry. Why? The reasons are varied. Sometimes a person will become fully convinced that you are evil (or abusive, or

> Wounded people are walking into your office and into your church with loaded emotional guns. They do not know the danger that is in their hands.

false, or incompetent, etc.[25]) and that you must be stopped in the name of Jesus. Another reason might be retaliation. (the person is attacking you because of an offense or a deep wound he or she has received). Other possible reasons involve issues of authority/control or acceptance/rejection, or relational closeness/distance. The turmoil that has been dormant within them for years has now been awakened. Their personal thunderstorm has been unleashed, and you're the one standing in the field holding a lightning rod. Whatever the reasons, I am warning you this will happen. Someone will make it his or her mission to take you down.

You may be surprised that these particular people have become advocates for your destruction. You would have never guessed that they would be attacking you in this way and with this level of intensity. Their words and actions seem incongruous, out of balance with the act that offended them. A deeper pain within their hearts has been uncovered, and you're the one who's going to get the full assault.

In such a case, assess the danger, and then confirm your assessment with your elders. Set a rigid boundary between you and those who are attacking you. Never meet alone with them. Never speak on the phone with them without a third party listening in. Always work with a witness at your side. Many pastors have lost their careers not because they sinned, but because they were careless concerning this boundary.

Boundaries in Communication

E-mails and Written Correspondence
At least once a year, preach a sermon on healthy communication. Remind your congregation that e-mail is one-way communication and is quite limiting in any conversation that has to do with relationships. Teach your people about the importance of face-to-face communication — how a great deal of a person's message comes through non-verbal cues such as facial expression, tone of voice, gestures, and posture. Clarification and the "give and take" of a conversation cannot be achieved in written correspondence. Offer examples (not from your own church) of hurtful e-mails that got rifled off in a moment of anger. This yearly sermon along with other forms of equipping constitute an important proactive measure against a very harmful and growing problem in church life.

As for yourself, limit what you write in letters and e-mails. Here is a good rule: Write only what you are comfortable with everyone in your church (or in the world) reading. E-mails will get forwarded. Do not be casual or lax with them. Save every important e-mail you write or receive. You never know when you will need to give an accounting for your words.

If you are corresponding via e-mail with a person whose relationship with you is complex (for example, it might be intense or conflicted), here are my suggestions concerning a path forward:

[1] Write to the person and explain that e-mail communication is limiting and is not the best way to have an important and heart-felt conversation. Let the person know that you are willing to have this discussion face-to-face, but not via e-mail.

[2] Communicate to the person that having another elder present can greatly enhance such a meeting. "Let's design our time together so that we're doing all we can to listen to one another and further the work of Christ."

[3] Propose a path forward: "Please call the office and let's schedule this meeting. If I don't hear from you in a week, I'll be contacting you. Getting together is important to me."

> *Here is a good rule: write only what you are comfortable with everyone in your church (or in the world) reading.*

For a person who continues to use e-mail inappropriately and won't adhere to the procedure outlined above, respond to their e-mail in the following way: "As I have stated before, I am willing to sit down with you and have this discussion, but am not willing to continue such a conversation through e-mail. Starting with the next e-mail, all correspondence that I send to you or receive from you will be copied/

forwarded to another elder so that a third party can help us in this communication."

Some members of your congregation will resent you for copying e-mails to a third-party, but I have found that it is a necessary (and the cleanest) practice in this medium of communication. A further note about e-mail: I do not like the "blind copy" feature. I always want to know who is receiving the communication I am reading, so I want to afford the recipient of my e-mails the same courtesy. In this way, you model healthy, straightforward communication within all your relationships.

Phone Conversations

The same principles hold true with phone conversations. Unless you are on conference call, there is no witness to the conversation you are having. Therefore, do not enter into deep or challenging discussions over the phone. Use the phone to design the proper environment to have the critical discussion.

Confidentiality

Reverence communication, but do not participate in secret-keeping. When someone begins to disclose sensitive information to you (*"I did something I'm very ashamed of."* or *"I'm planning on taking an action that no one else knows about yet."*), interrupt them. Explain that you are willing to listen and help him or her walk with integrity and accomplish the Lord's purposes. In order to accomplish this, you may not be able to keep secret what they are about to disclose. If the information about to be shared causes you to believe the person speaking or someone else might be in danger, then you have an ethical, moral, and legal responsibility to intervene and include other people in the discussion.

Otherwise, what will you do when you have vowed to keep a secret and the person tells you they are contemplating suicide? What will you do when the person discloses his or her marital infidelity? Beware, or you will find yourself caught in this communication trap.

> *Reverence communication but do not participate in secret-keeping.*

Never promise to keep secrets. Be a trustworthy pastor who ministers lovingly and respectfully concerning the brokenness of others, but do not get trapped in the snare of secret-keeping.

Moving Forward

Competence in the area of boundary setting (or the lack of it) can make or break a pastor's career. Whether in the domain of communication, schedule, or friendship, be vigilant in guarding the doorways of your life and ministry. Be aware that most people are not cognizant of the subtle principles of healthy boundaries; at times they cross lines inappropriately without even knowing it. When it happens, approach it the same as driving a car defensively; another driver at the intersection might choose to do something crazy, so keep your eyes open. As you maintain biblical boundaries, your congregation will learn and benefit from your example. Check your doors and gates. Make sure they are functioning properly, so that you can live out your calling in the power of the Spirit!

I have set you an example that you should do
as I have done for you.
John 13:15

Survival Key #6
Know How to Lead

One of my elders began to engage in divisive conversations with key members of the congregation. None of the other leaders saw this coming—all of us had believed this elder was a person of character and integrity. The leadership team confronted him, but he refused to stop. Though this elder was dismissed, great damage was done to the church. Members were put in a position of having to choose whom they believed. Many people refused to take a position and simply left the church.

—Anonymous

Paul and Barnabas appointed elders for them in each church and, with prayer and fasting, committed them to the Lord, in whom they had put their trust.

— Acts 14:23

Do not be hasty in the laying on of hands. . .
— 1 Timothy 5:22

Power, Authority and Leadership

I've heard it said that where two or three people are gathered together, there is a struggle for power. This is true not only in the secular world, but also within the church. You must be very aware of power and authority issues within yourself, within others, and in the systems and services of the church.

What should church leadership look like? It should be servant-like in attitude (Phil.2:5-7), plural in form (Titus1:5, Acts 14:23), mature in character (1 Tim.3:1-7; Titus 1:5-9), unified in purpose (Phil.2:2-4), biblical in thinking (2Tim.2:15), and courageous in leading (1Pe.5:1-4). The team must be committed to Kingdom ministry. Decisions should be made by consensus. Every member must have a voice, as well as being a team player (open to correction, not easily offended, teachable) and having only one agenda: To hear from God and obey His direction.

Every year, many churches split apart or shut down due to the misuse of power, poor management style, or a lack of team mentality among leaders. Do not think for a minute that any pastor is immune from this danger. God has called you to minister within community and accountability. I believe that the authority of a local church ultimately resides in the elder team, led by the pastor. You need a team. Even in your best moments, you have blindness and limited understanding. Gather around yourself a leadership team that will assist you in discovering God's prophetic direction for your church.

The domain of leadership is explosive. Get it right and your church will flourish. Get it wrong and your church and your ministry could be destroyed.

A Pastor's Authority

To walk in your true authority as a pastor, you must first settle the primary authority issue in your own life. Who is on the throne of your heart? If your feelings, opinions, wisdom or personal agendas drive you, your heart has shifted from being Christ-governed to being self-governed. When the enemy sees the lack of complete surrender in a pastor's heart, it is then he will pounce. Do not give him any ground. Remember survival key number one, and be absolutely vigilant concerning the posture of your own heart. Only then can you walk in your authority as pastor of the church. What does this look like?

In their book, *The Subtle Power of Spiritual Abuse*, David Johnson and Jeff VanVonderen wrote, "Spiritual abuse can occur when a leader uses his or her spiritual position to control or dominate another person. It often involves overriding the feelings and opinions of another, without regard to what will result in the other person's state of living, emotions or spiritual well-being."[26]

"Power over" leadership is not biblical. We are not called to be the Caesars of a kingdom, but servants of the King. Some pastors are on power trips, loving the attention of being the so-called "head." Any use of the pastoral office to coerce, impose, or manipulate is an abuse of power and is not of the Spirit of God.

On the other hand, I can tell you from experience that a vacuum of authority is just as dangerous as an over-reaching/controlling authority. When a pastor does not lead, others will attempt to fill the void. Anarchy comes in a variety of forms, none of them are good. More importantly, no form of anarchy is biblical. God has called you to lead in your church. Until that call changes, do so gently but without apology.

There is a grasping for power: like the first Adam who reached out to be like God. Then there is a power that surrenders, like the second Adam, "who in very nature God, did not consider equality with God something to be grasped" (Phil.2:6). Do not grasp! At the same time, do not abdicate your position of authority and step away from the place where the Spirit has you standing.

> *Learn all you can about how power operates in systems. In this way, you can help prevent abuse, manipulation and other destructive uses of power in relationship.*

You will need to develop a high level of discernment with regard to issues of power and authority. Some people crave it, others fear it, but every person is impacted by it. Learn all you can about how power operates in systems. Become a student of its subtleties. In this way, you can help prevent abuse, manipulation, and other destructive uses of power in relationship.

True spiritual authority is not haughty and loud. It is not about theological degrees or the titles on a business card. It is derived from a life hidden in Christ and lived out in strict obedience to God's call. Those who are not spiritually discerning will not honor true authority no matter what you do. I'm saying this to you now so that when you are disrespected without cause, you will not be discouraged. However, people who are grounded in the Word will respect this kind of spiritual authority and will not settle for the worldly counterpart.

The Role and Appointment of Elders

When the time has come to add elders to your team, do not vote. This is not a political process. Rather, appoint elders as per Titus 1:5, Acts 14:23. Have your current elder team set forth candidates. Be extremely careful and prayerful in choosing these candidates because your decision will set the table for years to come.

Do you have any true elders in your church? You can spot them quickly if you do. There is a statesmanship, a level of spiritual maturity that a discerning person can recognize even when walking into a church for the first time. This takes discernment because there is a subtle destructiveness in leaders who may be very gifted but are unable to loosen their hands from their agendas instead of offering themselves fully to the cause of Christ.

Perhaps your denomination has a particular process that must be followed. As for my counsel, here are the basic principles I see in Scripture and have learned in my years of ministry:

[1] Required character qualities of an elder are essential (1 Tim.3:1-7; Titus 1:5-9). Take them seriously. Though a person may have leadership gifts, he or she may not exhibit the "fruit of the Spirit" (Gal.5:22-23), which can be formed only through consistent abiding in Christ. In order to see the true character of a person, you must walk with that person for a period of time (at least two years). It is important to see the elder candidate in tense, emotionally-filled situations. You can truly tell what's in the heart of a person when he or she is squeezed.

[2] A personal relationship with Jesus, a mature theology, and a solid knowledge of the Bible. Intimacy with the Lord is essential. A love for the Word is essential. I look carefully not only at candidates' faith convictions, but also at their hermeneutic. Do they have a consistent methodology in interpreting Scripture? Do they have a developed systematic theology? These tools are foundational in order for a person to be an effective elder.

[3] A solid sense of self. Potential candidates cannot draw their identity from the opinions of others. They must be principled people of conviction, certain of their identity and destiny in Christ.

[4] A willingness to mutually submit to other leaders and to be part of a team. It is not possible to overemphasize this point, so please take it to heart. People who are unwilling to hear other perspectives can destroy a church more quickly than anyone else.

I'd rather have a witch standing outside the door of our church speaking curses over our ministry than to have a self-agendized leader at the elder table. Such leaders are arrogant, self-righteous, and extremely dangerous. An elder who is unwilling to serve on a team and prayerfully consider the counsel of other leaders can bring about the destruction of a church. He or she has been given spiritual authority in the church. Such lack of submission will lead to division and destruction. Do not place a candidate into leadership who doesn't understand and practice submission and humility.

[5] An earnest desire to serve the church as a shepherd. Unless a candidate truly wants to equip and serve people, that person is not ready to be an elder.

[6] An ability and giftedness to move as an overseer in the church. The gift set required of an overseer includes the ability to listen, to reason, and to consider prayerfully various options. There may be some wonderful people who are called to lead powerful and important ministries in the church, but who are not called to the work of an overseer/elder.

Once candidates have been selected and appointments have been announced to the church, allow a time of testing (in our church, it is two weeks) during which congregational members might bring questions or concerns before the candidates. The church must be certain that the candidate is a person of character and has a calling to be an overseer. That being said, it should be clear that each appointment is confirmed not by the congregation, but by your current elder team. I would also suggest an agreed-upon list of expectations for new elders and a time of testing (perhaps the first year) to see whether or not the person truly is ready and able to handle the responsibility.

Leadership Development

The real testimony of mature church leadership is when the church continues to thrive even when the pastor is absent. In order for this to occur, the elders must become vision-bearers, not just vision-repeaters. They must be trail-blazers, working right beside you for the Kingdom of God.

Spend time developing and caring for your leaders. Pay close and consistent attention to your staff, your elders, and your deacons. The faithful co-workers that God has brought you are your most valu-able resource. For most of my ministry, I was drawn to the "squeaky wheel," or to the sudden "brush-fires" breaking out in the congregation. The urgent requires some attention, but caregiving and pouring into those who are faithfully serving became one of my key priorities. The battle is great in the lives of people dedicated to the Lord's work. Do not believe the lie that because a leader is not complaining he or she does not need prayer or encouragement. Pay close attention to the health of your key ministry leaders. They are the multipliers and equippers of the church. Satan wants nothing more than to destroy the key workers and visionaries whom God has placed around you.

Spend time with each of your elders on a consistent basis (even once a month for an hour is a positive contribution). During that hour-long conversation, do not discuss church matters. Rather, focus on that elder's life and spiritual development. Take time to bless, encourage, listen, and pray for each leader in your church.

Invest in elder team development. Schedule two elder retreats a year. These need not be three- day, two- night events. Even spending six hours as a team outside the church building can be effective for team-building and transformation. Make it a priority to come alongside of your elders. Keep your eyes on the relational dynamics of your team. One strategy of the enemy is to divide and conquer. Satan will attempt to isolate a particular elder from the rest of the team. Be proactive! Don't wait until your team is broken beyond repair. Be courageous to address any avoidance, disconnection, relational distance, or resentments. By leading in this way, you establish a line of defense for the inner circle of your church, thus protecting it from the enemy's primary plan of attack.

Leadership Monday through Friday

The ministry that takes place behind the scenes from Monday to Friday sets the stage for your corporate worship and prayer services. You need a strategic plan to navigate the organizational and relational complexities of your day-to-day pastoral respon-sibilities. Here is what I've learned in my years of ministry:

Administration

Administration (which literally means "pre-ministry") sets the table for all the functions within your church. It is an extremely important task, one that you should delegate. Appoint people who are "full of the Holy Spirit and wisdom" (Acts 6:3). They also need to be humble servants, and willing to submit to elder authority.

As for you, the rule in this area is *eyes on, but hands off*. Though this area requires your vision, do not become over-involved with administrative details. Your main calling is to focus not on specifics, but on prophetic vision. The Apostles of the early church realized this spiritual truth: "It would not be right for us to neglect the ministry of the word of God in order to wait on tables. Brothers, choose seven men from among you who are known to be full of the Spirit and wisdom. We will turn this responsibility over to them and will give our attention to prayer and the ministry of the word" (Acts 6:2-4).

Staff Relationships

Nearly every denomination has its own struc-ture concerning staff reporting and accountability. If you are free to choose a structure, I believe it is best for all *ministry* staff (not administrative and support staff) to report to the pastor and for the pastor to be accountable to the elders. Under such a construct, you will be someone's *boss and pastor*—a very complex terrain indeed. Victory on this battlefield will depend on your adopting true definitions of these terms and breaking the false ones. Being the boss does not mean you're an authoritarian tyrant; being the pastor does not mean you never set a deadline. Being the boss does not mean that you're more concerned about tasks than you are about people. Being the pastor does not mean that you will always choose people over tasks.

It is essential that you set the ground rules and expectations for all working relationships. Job descriptions, policies, and procedures must be clearly articulated by the elders and written in your articles of incorporation or church charter. Every member of your staff should have a yearly review in which the elders participate. This important meeting should not only focus upon the previous year, but should set forth expectations and goals for the next.

I suggest that you schedule a quarterly meeting with each member of your staff in order to discuss the progress he or she is making on their ministry objectives for the year. Don't be afraid to set deadlines as a result of what you hear in these meetings. Intervene more directly if the situation warrants. If one of your staff members is struggling with administration or finances or communication, ask one of your elders who is competent in that area to come alongside to equip and support. You gain substantial ground when you choose to be straight and honest with your staff. Say what you need to say in your meetings. Any correction should be done in private and with the person's dignity in mind.

Your staff is working under your watch; they are not independent contractors. Do not micro-manage, but manage. In every ministry area, make sure healthy goals are set and that people are working diligently to accomplish them.

If others (custodians, secretaries, etc.) have access to your office, make sure no sensitive information is left on your desk. Do not leave your journal or elder notes in the sanctuary or lying around in your office. Secretaries and administrative assistants may inadvertently become privy to sensitive information as they work in your office. Design systems that help maintain healthy information boundaries. Also, be careful about the reactions you show and the words you say in the more relaxed office environment. Your staff will most likely change over time, so portray in the office the same demeanor, integrity, and character that characterize your public ministry.

Elder Team Meetings

I meet with my elders once a week for two hours. The weekly agenda can be a battleground. The urgent always screams for attention. Try not to get trapped in spending too much time on the administrative work of the church (this is more the task of the staff). Learn to delegate so that you can move forward with essential elder discussions on such topics as shepherding, direction, the Word, and prayer. After praying, look over the agenda and start with the items that you and your team feel are of utmost priority.

Remember to include items that focus on God's prophetic direction and the enemy's attacks. Seek consensus in decision-making. Encourage all members of the team to speak their hearts and to leave everything at the table. If the discussion gets bogged down, step away from it, pray together, and try again. The tendency will always be to trust your own understanding. Learn to use your spiritual gifts and weaponry.

As noted earlier in this chapter, the enemy will constantly attack the unity of your elder team. Be alert to subtle changes in the relational dynamics; have a keen eye for anyone distancing themselves from the team. Push to resolve unsettled discussions and hurt feelings. Don't allow distance to creep in.

There will be seasons when a particular elder frustrates you. Do not speak inappropriately about this leader, even to someone else on the team. Be careful how you express your frustration. Go directly to the elder with whom you're struggling. Treat every person the way you would want to be treated. Have the conversations you need to have, but have them in a straightforward and honoring way. Walk with integrity.

Don't be sloppy and casual. Rather, be professional and full of light. Prepare for your elder meetings. Awaken and inspire your team. Bring prophetic insight. Suggest books that provoke and challenge new thought. Stir up the gifts of your team. Encourage them; they are the heart of your church.

Shepherding

Pastor, you cannot be overly concerned what your congregation thinks of you. Do not allow angry words, teary eyes, or downcast faces to direct your ministry interventions. You are called to shepherd. You cannot back away from your call. Protect the flock (no matter what the personal cost), feed the sheep (even when they are too lazy to eat), lead them to the waters (even when they fight your leadership). The owner of the sheep has given you a job. You are to obey Him and not the sheep.

> *The Owner of the sheep has given you a job. You are to obey Him and not the sheep.*

Do not misrepresent what I am saying. Abusive speech and controlling leadership are sinful and wholly unacceptable. You are to be gentle, kind, and full of the Spirit of God. However, fulfill your calling as a shepherd even when your interventions are not met with applause.

Shepherd the shepherds

The daily work of a pastor is enormous. Do not think, even for a moment, that you can shepherd the flock all by yourself! Produce producers. Mentor those who will someday mentor others. Practice God's math by exchanging addition for multiplication in your ministry.

Consider what I am saying in terms of discipleship. If I mentor one hundred people in the course of my life and they continue to follow the Lord, then

I've empowered one hundred people to Kingdom work. Not bad. However, if I mentor ten people who, in the following year, mentor three people each, and each group multiplies annually in the same way—look at the shift:

Year One: ten new disciples for the Kingdom
Year Two: 30 new disciples for the Kingdom
Year Three: 90.
Year Four: 270.
Year Five: 810.

In this example, addition (and superhuman effort) harvested one hundred laborers. Multiplication (and Holy Spirit power) harvested hundreds more. Don't be content to add; multiply! Empower and teach others to empower. Mentor and teach others to mentor. In order to do this, you must be willing to relinquish control and not be the center of every endeavor. Release people fully and watch how the work increases! Give it away for the sake of Christ!

Multi-apply! This thinking must be applied laterally and in many domains. One of your goals should be about reproducing a variety of ministries everywhere. When someone is ready to receive Christ, allow someone who has never led a person in the prayer of salvation to take that opportunity instead of you. It is a blessing for you to lead someone to Christ, but it will be absolutely transforming for your friend who has never done it! Equip people to lead a prayer service or the new Bible study—then release them to lead in their own way. A mature, biblically-oriented leader is always thinking this way.

Let me say it again: You cannot personally minister to every need of every individual in your congregation. God did not design the church in this way. At the outset of your ministry (or as soon as possible if it's too late for that), find people in your congregation who have pastoral/shepherding gifts. Some people are willing to get up in the middle of night to help someone in need. Pull these individuals aside and ask if they would be willing to participate in a care-giving ministry under your direction. Furthermore, create one-anothering ministries under the five fold equipping model of Ephesians 4:11-13. Keep in mind, however, that your congregation will be noticing everything you're doing (and not doing). Therefore, pay attention to following basic relational principles:

[1] Be kind to people. Jesus loves every person, so treat every person with dignity and respect. I've met very talented and gifted pastors who are not nice people. Nobody likes a mean, grumpy pastor, even if he or she can preach a great sermon. Humility and simple kindness are powerful attributes in the spiritual realm.

[2] Do a lot of listening. Active listening is rare. Be counted among the few pastors who actually practice this artful ministry. When we talk all the time, we are relinquishing a powerful ministry tool.

[3] Be honest with people. People of integrity (words and actions matching) will follow a pastor of integrity.

[4] Exhibit courage. Stand with people and, when necessary, set yourself over against them on their behalf.

[5] Earnestly seek God's prophetic direction. Reading the Bible is not enough. There is no verse in the Bible that tells you whether or not to purchase a building for your church. There is no verse in the Bible that tells you whether or not to hire the youth pastor you just interviewed. A pastor must hear the Lord's direction for his or her life and ministry.

What do I mean by the prophetic? I am speaking about specific counsel and direction from the Spirit. "And in the church God has appointed first of all apostles, second prophets, third teachers. . ." (1Cor.12:28). The order here is important. First is the apostolic, which refers to the teachings of the Bible. God will never direct a church to move outside the counsel of Scriptures. Second is the prophetic. There is a more specific direction (never outside the sphere of the apostolic teaching) that will bring about necessary transition within the life of the church. Once the prophetic is discovered in a particular season, begin to teach it systematically.

Pastoral Counseling

Pastoral counseling is not therapy. My advice is that you do not enter into any in-depth counseling (more than two or three sessions) with members of your church. Even if you are trained in counseling, this is a dangerous line to cross. My reasoning for this is best understood in terms of relational dynamics.

Therapy enters into vulnerable and deep battlefields of a person's life. You may be able to separate your counseling role from your shepherding role, but what if your client/parishioner cannot? What if he or she becomes embarrassed to see you on a Sunday morning because of what was disclosed during the last counseling session? Regardless how well you can boundary your roles, regardless of your skill in counseling, your relationship with your congregant will change because of the depth of sharing in therapy.

Furthermore, good therapy is risky. Healing is very close to the pain. At times, clients may strike out and blame the therapist for their pain. If the therapist is the pastor, then conflicted parishioners may not only terminate the relationship with your counseling office but also with your church. Very suddenly, wounded sheep can lose two vital support systems.

Do not get caught in this trap. Shepherd hurting people by helping them find good Christian counseling. Then walk with them, not in the specifics of their journey, but more generally, displaying concern and offering support.

Other Churches in Your Community

Become acquainted with other pastors in your town. Even if it takes you three years, go to every church nearby and spend an hour thanking the pastor and the staff of that church for the ministry they provide for the community and the Body of Christ.

Let your church be known as a church that blesses and works with other churches.

Further relational development is essential. Find at least two or three pastors that you connect with theologically and relationally, and schedule regular meetings once or twice a month. This resource is invaluable; those who are walking the same trail as you and can prove to be helpful allies in survival.

Make every effort to establish deeper relation-ships with pastors of different ethnic backgrounds. Every person in the world has some level of cultural blindness. Some of the deepest assumptions we have about God, ourselves, others, ministry and life will remain unchallenged apart from racially-diverse relationships.

Ecumenism is a term and a ministry philosophy that must be defined carefully. Our Lord desires churches to work together for the advancement of the Kingdom of God, but close partnerships with some churches may be detrimental to the specific calling the Lord has for your congregation.

In areas of social justice (speaking out against discrimination, injustice, inequities, abuse, etc) and relief work in your community (feeding the hungry, ministry to victims of flooding or fire, homelessness, etc.) it is good to establish a broad alliance with as many churches as possible.

For more *general* community worship and prayer gatherings (when the purpose of the gathering is a time of prayer for the nation, a Thanksgiving Service, a prayer service on Martin Luther King, Jr. Day, etc), it is important for your church to set aside some of its normal, corporate practices (whether it be worship styles, the corporate expression of spiritual gifts, certain liturgical expectations) and participate. Perhaps even some peripheral doctrinal distinctives must be set aside for the sake of unity. Don't worry. You will not be struck down by lightning if you choose to meet once a year with other congregations that may not share your views about politics or prayer language. For too long, labels such as Protestant, Catholic, dispensational, Pentecostal fundamentalist, charismatic, liberal and conservative, have prevented the church universal from gathering in the name of Christ.

At the same time, I suggest that you participate only in *Christian* worship services. By this I mean that the central doctrines of biblical Christianity are agreed upon and taught. Not all churches (even those that have "Christian" in their name) believe that Jesus is Lord and that His atoning work on the cross is the only way for humankind to be reconciled to the Creator God. Some churches are offended by this foundational principle of orthodox Christianity; they feel such a position is arrogant and exclusive.

Promote unity and establish ties in the greater Body of Christ. Work with other churches to bless people and serve the community. However, be careful with whom you develop deeper partnerships. If you can find two or three pastors that you really trust and who journey with you in prayer, you have truly been blessed.

Moving Forward

Whether in corporate worship services or in your daily work among your congregation, constantly be aware of the dynamics of power and authority within your church. Remember that many people have been hurt and even abused by people in positions of authority, so don't be surprised if some of your parishioners struggle to trust you and your elders. It takes a strong sense of identity and tremendous perseverance to be successful on this battlefield, but this is strategic terrain that must be taken in the name of Christ. Continue to exemplify servant leadership without abdicating God's call on your life to shepherd the flock. As you walk in this manner, you will be living out true biblical leadership and leading your congregation in a counter-cultural and life-giving way.

So Christ Himself gave the apostles, the prophets,
the evangelists, the pastors and teachers, to equip
His people for works of service, so that the body of
Christ may be built up until we all reach unity in
the faith and in the knowledge of the Son of God
and become mature, attaining to the whole
measure of the fullness of Christ.
Ephesians 4:11-13

Survival Key #7
Know Your Mission

Most of my training prepared me for the one hour on Sunday morning.
— Leith Anderson, senior pastor of Wooddale Church in Eden Prairie, MN[27]

For the first five or six years of my pastoral ministry, my main goal was to walk with people and care for them. I began to realize that I was called to more than simply helping people adjust to different stages of their lives. I knew the Bible spoke of serving others; I just didn't know how to move the church in that direction. No one mentored me in how to break the bondages of self-absorption and entitlement within a congregation and liberate the church into mission. I wanted it; I just didn't know how to get there.
— Anonymous

What are we doing?

Especially in America, we have lost the vision of the Kingdom of God. We have found the path of least resistance, and Christianity has become Churchianity, so to speak. We've become self-absorbed, and many people walk into church saying, "This is what I want: I want good music, a twenty-minute sermon, a few people to greet me, and then be home in an hour. I don't really want investment, I don't want deep relationships, I don't have margin for anything else. I want a church that fits my life."

I think God has something better for us than this myopic self-absorption, this entitled Christianity. He wants to place a new vision at the doorposts of our homes and on the tablets of our hearts, and it is about His Kingdom. He wants us to invest in His Kingdom.

In the words of John Wesley, "Give me one hundred preachers who fear nothing but sin and desire nothing but God...such alone will shake the gates of hell and set up the Kingdom of heaven on earth."

Your Mission Part One: In Your Church

Prepare for advancement into the world by advancing the following strategies within your church:

[1] Establish a prayer base.
[2] Pursue prophetic worship and preaching.
[3] Equip the saints by utilizing the five-fold equipping gifts of Ephesians 4:11-13.

Establish a Prayer Base

Do you have two or three true intercessors in your community? If so, you have truly been blessed by the Lord! Call on them and ask them to pray for your survival. Ask them to intercede daily for you, your family, your elder team and the church. This is the initial hedge of protection in the spiritual realm. From this beginning point, you can extend outward and advance for His glory. Meet with this small team weekly. Encourage them. Give them general prayer points. Pour into them. The Lord has placed them as your guards in the spiritual realm.

Prayer is the deepest, most intimate spiritual discipline. When this work is being accomplished in your church, ministry begins to accelerate, but so do the attacks. The enemy is not concerned with plastic Christianity, but when believers fall on their knees and cry out desperately for God's Kingdom to come, the demons are stirred up like a hornet's nest.

The "simple" decision to establish a prayer service is huge in the spiritual realm. Attacks will come from every direction. You have set a stake and the enemy will snarl at you. You have made a declaration to move forward into the battle and not play church.

There are very few praying churches in the world. Many pastors preach on the importance of prayer, and many books have been written about it, but few churches truly practice it. Many seem to be thriving because thousands of people attend Sunday morning worship, yet only twenty people attend the weekly prayer meeting. Such a discrepancy reveals the depth of a church's commitment to God.

> You can tell how popular a church is by who comes on Sunday morning. You can tell how popular the pastor or evangelist is by who comes on Sunday night. But you can tell how popular Jesus is by who comes to the prayer meeting.
> —guest speaker in Jim Cymbala's church[28]

There are churches that are willing to meet in a field in the middle of winter in order to hear the Word being preached. Other churches will cancel a service because it's Super Bowl Sunday. Some Christians fast for weeks, praying that they might receive a Bible of their own. Other Christians leave in the middle of a sermon because it is past lunchtime and they're not going to wait any longer. What makes the difference? One Christian has become convinced that apart from

God's intervention his life will amount to nothing. The other Christian believes the gospel is optional and doesn't need to be fully embraced.

Do we really believe that apart from Him we can do nothing? Do we really believe that intimacy with Christ is at the heart of transformation? Such conviction will drive us to our knees and we will devote ourselves to the wonderful discipline of prayer. At the very beginning of your ministry, decide that your church will be a praying church.

Prayer times open our eyes to the truth about God and the truth about ourselves: that God is great and we are not. We need Him. A mindset of desperation begins to emerge within a praying church. Choose this day to be a pastor who both practices and promotes prayer. Apart from the Spirit of God we can do nothing of eternal consequence.

Church Leadership and Prayer

Your elders and deacons must be fully on board and willing to commit themselves to this prayer time. They need to be present. If you preach that prayer is important but your leaders don't actually come to the meeting, no one will believe you. I recommend that the elders and deacons of the church already be present and praying before the meeting begins. There is something powerful about seeing an entire leadership team kneeling at the altar and interceding for the church and for God's mission in the world. People will respect and follow that kind of leadership.

A unified leadership team that is committed to prayer doesn't develop overnight. Don't be surprised

when you find resistance from an elder or a deacon.
The arguments can be articulate and reasonable:

> *"People are so busy! We don't want to
> overburden them."*
> *"I can't commit to everything; I need to
> have time to minister to my family."*
> *"Of course prayer is important, but why
> do we need to come together? Why can't we all
> pray individually from our homes as God calls
> us to pray?"*

Keep your position simple and steadfast: God
desires us to be a praying community (Lk.19:46, Acts
2:42, 1Thess.5:17). God has called us to establish a
corporate prayer meeting. The culture of the church
will not change apart from the community moving
together. It pleases God when we gather in His name
to seek His face.

Through these conversations with your leaders
(and such discussions may continue on for months
and months), you will begin to see each person's willingness to walk with you on this journey. Everyone in
the room believes prayer is good! It is not a theological issue; it is a question of commitment and convenience. You will probably see a change in leadership
through this time. Pray that it doesn't destroy your
church. Establishing prayer in your church is often
costly, but in the end, our churches will amount to
nothing apart from prayer. What good is it to have a
mega-church but no warriors? Fight this battle to gain

the beachhead of prayer. Then, move to advance the Kingdom of God with the power of the Holy Spirit!

Structuring the Weekly Prayer Meeting

Prayer services are strategic for advancement, so expect the enemy to interfere any way he can. Typical methods are distraction, offense, carnal spirituality and tardiness. To diffuse them, prepare for your prayer meetings ahead of time. Ask your elders and your key intercessors to join you thirty minutes before the service begins. Have an "agenda" for the prayer meeting, but always leave space for something unexpected. Place prayer needs on PowerPoint or overheads. Break out of the traditional "one at a time" praying method and ask people to intercede all at once for the any of the requests before them.

I believe it is important to pray over particular domains of ministry. The structure of a prayer meeting will, in and of itself, be instructional for your congregation. Think in terms of: [1] personal transformation, [2] church transformation and [3] societal and global transformation.

Open with global as often as possible because it is healthy to begin with an outward focus. Take five or ten minutes and pray for your missionaries overseas, a local outreach of your church, a persecuted country, or a current crisis situation in the world (earthquake, flood, famine).

> *Linger in worship and adoration like Mary and intercede with the rigor of Martha.*

Church transformation might include prayer for small groups, for church leadership, for the youth or college ministry. Every ministry that exists in our churches needs to be bathed in prayer. All three areas of transformation may not be covered every week, so it is important to rotate through the month, as all these areas are vital and need consistent intercession.

It is important that people who are requesting prayer receive it at some point in the prayer meeting. Mobilize the priesthood to pray over the needs of the body. Prayer meetings are an excellent venue for practicing spiritual gifts, so encourage everyone to utilize what the Spirit has given them for the building up of the church. Instruct your congregation in the principle of take and give by saying, "This week, you may need to receive. Next week, perhaps you will be the one who can give." Both are valid parts of ministry.

Beyond this structure, add in worship and a time of waiting on the Lord. Give brief instruction on what you're looking for at particular times in the prayer meeting. Sometimes people want to move as a unit but just don't know what to do, so give them clear expectations and boundaries.

In the weekly prayer service, it is important to talk less and pray more. The reason you are gathered is to meet with God as a church. Pray for His manifest Presence to fill the sanctuary. Jesus is interceding for each of us in the heavenly tabernacle. Strive to hear His prayers and then pray them for one another according to the Spirit. Beware of people who want to dominate the prayer time. Instruct your congrega

> *Be intentional in guarding an environment of "non-rush." Less talk; more space.*

tion not to "fill" the time with many things. Linger in worship and adoration like Mary and intercede with the rigor of Martha. Always remember that worship and prayer perform a beautiful sacred dance before the King of Kings.

Monthly Prayer Vigils

I have learned from our African brothers and sisters how powerful an extended time of prayer can be for my church community and our outreaches. By "extended," I mean starting with at least four hours of prayer. Then, over the first few months, quickly lengthen the vigils. Try a twelve hour vigil one day. Later, try one that extends through the night. Intersperse prayer times with worship. Include all types of prayer; don't be afraid to stretch and experiment.

Prayer before the Services

Prayer before Sunday worship or any corporate service is essential to changing the mindset of ministry from self-sufficiency to God-dependency. Over time, people will begin to catch the vision of coming early and being spiritually prepared. Of course, this will happen only if the leadership is first committed to the practice and discipline of prayer.

Pursue Prophetic Worship and Preaching

For years, all of us have experienced church services that are organized and directed in a certain way. Have these services brought real transformation? For years, we have seen committed church members participating in worship singing and listening to biblical sermons. The question is: Are mature and powerful warriors for the Kingdom being developed from all of our labor? Compare the church in the Book of Acts with our churches today. The first century church had such life and power and faith. How much of that do we see in our communities today? Why perpetuate a system that doesn't bear fruit? In order to move in a fruitful way, pastors must think and act differently.

There are essential ingredients of a service: worship, prayer, the exercise of spiritual gifts, the ministry of the Word, the Sacraments, fellowship and the tithe. However, gathering is not primarily about doing; rather, it is about *meeting relationally* with God and with other believers. There is a difference between having a business meeting and meeting with a friend. A good business meeting follows an agenda and is about accomplishing a task. When two friends meet, it is about lingering, connecting and discovering. "Doing" is a part of the worship service, but Mary won over the Lord's favor when she simply lingered with Him, "seated at His feet" (Lk.10:39).

Be purposeful in lingering during worship services. Eliminate endless chatter. Who wants to hear fifteen minutes of announcements? Why preach a forty minute sermon if it can be shared in twenty minutes? Be intentional in cultivating an environment of "non-rush." We are a culture of many words. Sometimes it seems like every second of the service is filled with syllables. Look around. People are in a daze. We might as well be lecturing on the growth stages of front yard shrubs for an hour (we would get the same level of response). Try something different. Less talk; more space. Stop explaining what to pray; just pray. Stop introducing every song. What a difference it would make if we would make a conscious effort to stop moving the muscles that govern our jaws (even if it is for three minutes).

Our main objective is to meet with the Lord as a church and to follow His lead. He is always with us, but when His manifest Presence begins to fill the sanctuary, allow Him to minister as He sees fit. The worship service is not primarily about singing or preaching; it is about entering into His Presence and following Him in ministry. It is imperative that we not complicate this, either in our minds or in our communication to the church. We need to state unapologetically that the church is on a mission to hear the voice of the Living Christ and to be transformed in His Presence. Do not deviate from this goal, not ever.

Prophetic Worship and the Arts

Praise and worship in many forms of artistic expression are wonderful pathways for the Holy Spirit to touch our hearts. Encourage the utilization and expansion of these gifts in your church. Excellence in presentation is important, but authenticity is the top priority. Often, people look at the outward appearance only, but "the Lord looks at the heart" of the artist (1Sam.16:7). Ultimately, our expressions of worship are for an audience of One.

Praise is a powerful battering ram that breaks down walls that separate us from God and from one another. When a congregation enters into praise, a declaration of the awesomeness of God and the wonders of His victory is released into the heavenlies. Regardless of circumstances, the community of faith must choose to praise the name of the Lord and be barrier-breakers in the spiritual realm.

Worship is listening, lingering and waiting. God desires to hold us against His chest. He longs for us to quiet ourselves enough to hear His heart beat for us and for the world. Do not be afraid to linger in your times of worship. Significant breakthroughs are possible in these quiet moments. What might take a person ten years to discover in counseling can be brought to light in ten seconds before the throne of the Most High God.

Pray that your praise and worship times will be soaked in the prophetic, that the veil is pulled away to reveal a clear sense of God's Presence and direction in the here and now. Like anything else, it will take time for such gifting to fully mature. Be patient. Keep stretching. Encourage people to step out and explore.

Spiritual Gifts in Corporate Services

The spiritual gifts, when released properly, can shift the direction of a service and impact the congregation immediately. We are instructed to practice the gifts listed in 1Cor.12:7-11 in a "fitting and orderly way" (1Cor.14:40), but what does that look like in a corporate worship or prayer service? Here is what I have discovered:

A family theorist by the name of Salvador Minuchin described three types of boundaries: rigid, open and clear. An example of a rigid boundary would be a cement wall around a property — a wall without gates. Nothing gets in, nothing gets out. An open boundary could be likened to a picket fence with a single picket every ten feet: *everything* gets in and out. A clear boundary is like a solid fence with a gate: access is possible, but permission to come and go *must be granted.*

I recommend a clear boundary concerning spiritual gifts during your worship services. A rigid system does not allow spiritual gifts to be shared (or only the pastor or elders are allowed to offer a prophetic word). Such a system limits God. A visitor might walk into your church next Sunday and offer a transforming, prophetic word, but a rigid boundary would prevent that word from being heard.

An open system concerning spiritual gifts allows anything to be shared at any time. Imagine a microphone available for anyone to walk forward and offer what they deem to be prophetic. Such a system does not protect the church from inappropriate (or even false) words.

A clear boundary offers access, but through a gate. I would suggest two of your elders being the gate. People who believe they have a picture, a prophetic word or a tongue must first submit their offering to your two elders and receive confirmation and direction before sharing what's on their hearts.

No system is without challenges, but I believe that what I have proposed is the most balanced in terms of the biblical principles of the priesthood of all believers and order in the service.

Preaching and Teaching

> Preaching is indispensable to Christianity. Without preaching, a necessary part of its authenticity has been lost. For Christianity is, in its very essence, a religion of the Word of God.
> —John Stott[29]

It is essential for pastors to be equipped sufficiently in biblical theology and biblical interpretation. Choose right now to be a student of the Bible and of proper principles of interpretation. Remember, false and aberrant teaching often emerges from sincere but ignorant hearts.

Study often and consistently. If we truly believe that the Bible is God's Word written in human words—that all Scripture is inspired by God, fully authoritative and trustworthy—then we would deem it worthy of the daily discipline of study.

Bible College or Seminary degrees mean nothing in the spiritual realm, nor do fancy theological terms and interesting sermon illustrations. Spiritual principles based on the Word of God are the key to power in ministry. Choose to be a pastor who "correctly handles the word of truth" (2 Tim.2:15). This will require a consistent hermeneutic.[30]

The key to transformational preaching is to connect the broad principles of Scriptures to the prophetic word of the moment. Struggle to find the word that releases people into the Presence of God and into His Kingdom work.

For years, I preached biblical sermons. People nodded in agreement. I received compliments about my insights and my pursuit of the deeper meanings within the text. Still, something was missing: hardly anyone was being *transformed.*

There came a moment when my eyes opened to this stunning truth: *Solid preaching and wonderful worship are not enough.* I realized that I do not have the power to change hearts — not even my own. I began to speak a new type of prayer. It was more desperate, more helpless. I cried out for the Holy Spirit to empower the worship and preaching and testimonies and whatever else would happen in the service that day.

I began to preach differently. I prepared with the same rigor—studying the text exegetically and working hard to quiet myself before the Word. But there was a cry in my heart for transformation. I didn't have to manufacture it. It was authentic.

Preaching that transforms somehow connects the head with the heart and the feet, but it is primarily about a vessel that has caught the fire of the Holy Spirit and is willing to burn before others. Work hard at biblical interpretation and seek the prophetic word for your congregation. But more than anything else, cry out desperately for the Holy Spirit to light you on fire!

Survival Strategies in Corporate Services

Corporate services are tricky for a pastor. Don't lose yourself in these meetings. Give enough direction to get the engine started. Make sure you set the expectations and boundaries, but then allow the priesthood to emerge in these meetings. Don't abdicate your place, but give space and breathing room for others to catch fire and minister in the power of the Spirit.

Is Jesus the head of your church or is he merely a symbolic figurehead? Many churches are not fulfilling all that God has for them because the pastor is unwilling to relinquish control. You must be willing to follow the Spirit's lead in ministry. Don't be surprised if the Holy Spirit directs you to lead a worship or prayer service in an untraditional, unfamiliar way. Rather, be surprised if He doesn't!

The Maker of both goats and of galaxies, the God who fashions no two snowflakes the same, has some creative ideas for ministry, so don't try to fit Him into a box. Comfort and familiarity are barriers that must be broken if your church is going to grow toward spiritual maturity. Concern over what something looks like or sounds like is peripheral in the spiritual realm. The goal is equip the saints for the purpose of advancing the Kingdom. The most efficient method for this equipping is to follow the principles of the Word and our Lord's promptings. (He knows what He's doing in ministry!)

Here are a few more thoughts about corporate services:

[1] Be yourself in Christ as you stand before your congregation. Do not put on a professional pastor's face. Have courage to be authentic. You can give only what you have, so practice your daily private disciplines and minister in the fullness of the Spirit.

[2] Be prepared, but not rehearsed. Come to the service burning with the prophetic word for the day. If you don't have it, be actively looking for it. It is the prophetic word that will light the service on fire.

[3] Be praying prayers like this before the service: "Jesus, You are alive and present here. My number one agenda is to bless You and follow Your lead in ministry. You know the heart of every person here. You know the prophetic word that will light hearts on fire. Lord, Your ways are higher than my ways. Show me Your way in this service. I will not settle for less. I will not give in to the pressures of pleasing people or following my own understanding in ministry."

[4] Remember that it's never just about one service; it's about equipping the saints for Kingdom work. Expand your perspective. Is the time together shifting people into a Kingdom mindset? Will some of your congregants be different a year from now

because of the spiritual work being done in the present moment? If God's equipping gifts are active in your church, your congregation will be released into their callings, built up, and brought to maturity.

The Call of God on Leadership: Equipping the Saints

The main calling of a pastor is to train and equip an army that will take back ground from the enemy and advance God's purposes in the world. How are you going to train and mobilize your army so that you can fulfill the objective of your commissioning?

The answer is not simply preaching biblical sermons, creating fellowship opportunities and offering expressive worship times. All of this is good, but equipping may or may not take place through the preaching of the Word (some seeds fall on the hard path and some find good soil). Equipping may or may not take place in anointed times of worship (one person responds to God's gentle whisper, another turns away). One person is blessed by the challenge and encouragement within a small group, another is disappointed and chooses to leave.

So how do you equip the saints? Here's my answer: Recruit the ones that are catching fire and fan the flame with the five- fold equipping gifts.

Recruitment
Offer the Word, prayer and fellowship to every person who walks through the doors of your church, but invest deeply only in the people who view

Kingdom advancement as their life goal. Where are these "invested" people? For certain, it is not everyone in your congregation. It may be 20% or 60% of your present congregation, but it will never be 100%. A healthy church will always attract seekers and curious observers who are open to listening to the recruitment speech but are not yet ready to sign on the dotted line.

Learn to discern the "soil condition" of a person's heart. Why pour your life into a person who is not willing to stand in the battle? Why spend months mentoring a person you know has not fully committed himself or herself to the reign of God? The Lord may call you to pour into someone even when you see his or her questionable commitment (consider Jesus and Judas Iscariot), but be careful in whom you invest.

In order to achieve your goal of mobilizing an army for Kingdom advancement, you need recruits. Potential recruits are people within your church who are beginning to light up with the fire of God. They are catching the vision of the Kingdom and coming to grips with the radical commitment of discipleship. They are teetering on the edge of making the all-or-nothing decision to become a Jesus-follower. You see it in their eyes after a sermon—they are pierced to the heart with conviction. You see the passion in their worship and hear the desperation in their prayers. These people are being stirred to a deeper intimacy with God and want to cooperate with the Lord (and with you) in ministering to others.

In order to become a recruit in God's spiritual army, a person must be willing to proclaim Jesus as Lord over every aspect of his or her life (and not just speak the words, but be willing to walk it out). They must be willing to cross the bridge of absolute surrender and then burn the bridge (no turning back). For the nominal Christian, discipleship, full surrender, practicing the spiritual disciplines and complete abandonment are all options to be considered. For the viable recruit, all of these are mandatory. These expectations must be made clear.

In the same way that untrained civilians are in grave danger on the battlefield, those in your congregation who are not fully surrendered to Christ and trained for war are in danger spiritually. Cry out for soldiers and when you find your recruits, train them for war. Consider Sunday morning as an opportunity for recruitment. The real growth of the church will take place with your recruits in discipleship, in the prayer meetings, on the streets, in the fasting, on the field. Recruits must come to grips with the biblical terms of discipleship: their lives are no longer their own. They have been bought with a price and are now living for the sake of the Kingdom. "No one serving as a soldier gets involved in civilian affairs—he wants to please his commanding officer" (2Tim.2:4).

Take heart: You will have recruits. It may not be as many as you expected and you might be surprised who moves forward and who doesn't. Praise God for every real recruit you have and pray for more. Make your appeal continuously and in many different ways. Be liberal in sowing seeds for recruitment. When a seed finds good soil, it's time to act. Get that person into boot camp.

Boot Camp

Put 80% of your ministry effort into equipping the recruits that you have and the remaining 20% into finding more. Design a training regiment with the goal that, upon graduating, recruits will be able to survive and thrive in Christian work (graduates will be able to swim on their own). I believe this "boot camp" should be at least eighteen months in length and that the training should be rigorous and the expectations high, especially in the first month

> *Put 80% of your effort into equipping the recruits that you have, and the remaining 20% into finding more.*

so that those who are posing will be exposed early on. Boot camp must equip the saint in mind, in heart and in life. The five-fold equipping gifts of Ephesians 4:11-13 are the essential tools in this transformative work.

The Five Coaches

Think of the five equipping gifts as coaches on a football team. Though Apostle, Prophet, Evangelist, Pastor and Teacher all have unique skills and particular areas of expertise in preparing the team, their goal is singular: put a winning team on the field of ministry. Most likely, there will be teams of people (not just one person) sharing each coaching responsibility.

Once these coaches are given freedom to train the team, the "army" within your congregation will become evident. Establish these coaches and let them stir the pot.

Teacher equips in systematic theology and biblical interpretation. It is time for Christians to actually be thinkers, not just repeaters.

Prophet works to "de-junk" and disentangle the saints from past hurts, vows and unbiblical mindsets. Roadblock clearing is a specialty of the prophetic gift.

Pastor comes alongside the saints with both the rod and the staff. This gift is leading and directing, feeding and protecting.

Evangelist challenges self-absorbed, lazy and entitled lifestyles. This outward focus gives us vision to give ourselves away for the sake of Kingdom advancement.

Those with apostolic gift press the church to consider multiplying (birthing, planting) and producing fruit beyond itself. They broaden the Kingdom vision in transhistorical and transcultural ways. Modern-day apostolic teaching is founded upon the *kerygma* and is characterized by a broad and deep understanding of the theology of the New Testament.

Moving Forward

Keep your primary objective at the forefront of your mind all the time: call forth, mobilize, train and lead a spiritual army that will continue the work our Lord began in His earthly ministry. We are called to "preach good news to the poor, proclaim freedom for the prisoners and recovery of sight for the blind, to release the oppressed and to proclaim the year of the Lord's favor" (Lk.4:18-19). Pastor, set your mind on this goal. Gather the equippers around you and start mobilizing your army for the sake of His Kingdom!

Your Mission Part Two: In the World

Then Jesus came to them and said, "All authority in heaven and on earth has been given to me. Therefore go and make disciples of all nations, baptizing them in the name of the Father and of the Son and of the Holy Spirit, and teaching them to obey everything I have commanded you. And surely I am with you always, to the very end of the age."
—Matthew 28:18-20

The Great Commission is not an option to be considered; it is a command to be obeyed.
—Hudson Taylor

Some wish to live within the sound of a chapel bell; I wish to run a rescue mission within a yard of hell. — C.T. Studd

This generation of Christians is responsible for this generation of souls on the earth!
— Keith Green

The mark of a great church is not its seating capacity, but its sending capacity.
— Mike Stachura

The Church must send or the church will end.
— Mendell Taylor

I look upon the world as my parish. — John Wesley

The Mindset of Advancement

We are called to come to the Lord and be refreshed. We are also called to go into a broken world and make disciples of all nations. This coming and going is a spiritual rhythm, a healthy balance of receiving and giving. The private equipping, refreshing and repair between you and the Lord in your inner sanctuary is vital. Getting out of your church and onto the streets is equally as vital. Eliminating one or the other damages the "*shalom*-balance" the Lord desires.

The posture of the Spirit-filled pastor is advancement. After you have learned how to stand in Christ and hold the ground He's given you, God is calling you to take new ground and, in so doing, to set the captives free. If you remain in your own castle simply protecting what you have, you become like the servant who buried his one talent.

Your mindset about safety must change. A conservative approach is not necessarily safer. A strategy of non-advancement is not necessarily less risky. When God calls us to advance, the safest plan is to advance. When God calls us to pull back, the safest plan is to pull back. It is less risky walking on the water with Jesus than remaining huddled under a blanket in the boat without Him.

With that said, it is imperative for every pastor to realize that advancement is the normal posture for the church. The enemy is always looking for ways to invade your castle. The best defense consists of a powerful offense that moves into his territory. Keep the enemy on the move by preaching the Word of God and developing an advancing army out of your congregation.

God is the original pioneer. He is on the move and wants you to move with Him. Some pastors become lethargic and comfortable as they grow older. After twenty or thirty years in ministry, these pastors should be the most outrageous, excited, Spirit-filled dreamers on the face of the earth. Instead, boredom has set in. They have put their ministry on cruise control and are taking their leisure. Their ministry has become like old manna—worm-ridden and without nourishment. I love meeting pastors who are chronologically older but have youthful hearts. They are captivated by God's love. They are not afraid to take adventures with the Lord.

Become captivated by a holy restlessness, thirsty for new terrain and new discoveries. Allow His wonderment to embrace your heart.

S T R E T C H in the way you relate to others. Are you married? Do you have children? When the Spirit of God releases you into a mindset of advancement, they will recognize the change immediately. Your desire to learn, to discover, to listen, to dream, to actively invest and pursue more

> *Become captivated by a holy restlessness, thirsty for new terrain and new discoveries. Allow His wonderment to embrace your heart.*

deeply will radically change the dynamics of your home life.

As the mindset of advancement becomes more pronounced in you, every relational system in the church will be impacted too: the elder team, the deacon team, the intercessors, the worship teams, the prophets, the teachers, the administrators. You will begin to hear the language and dreams of advancement rising up in their conversations. That's when you know the new wine is finally being caught in something other than the old, inflexible wineskins.

The mindset of advancement is exciting, but there is a cost. In order to advance, you must be willing to leave the old and let go of the familiar. When you change the dance steps, some people won't like it. You might not like it either. It's like hiking a new trail; you don't know exactly what comes next, or what you will find around the next bend. It could lead to the most incredible view ever or you could get lost and have to retrace your steps. To advance, you must be willing to risk.

But there is also a significant cost that comes with a mindset of non-advancement. While you are working hard to protect and maintain the status quo of your life and ministry, your heart is dying a slow death—the death of non-adventure that comes from breathing stale spiritual air.

Jesus said, "Whoever wants to save his life will lose it, but whoever loses his life for me will save it" (Lk.9:24). God is calling you to advance outside the castle of your status quo life and ministry. Stop spending all your time protecting what you have.

Instead, give yourself away. Adventure with God. Journey with Him in the wild terrain. Breathe in the fresh air. Chase after the Poem that can only be heard outside the confines of the castle gate.

Develop also a mindset of advancement concerning your own personhood. Be open to new experiences in your daily journey with the Lord. Allow God's creativity to breathe life into your spiritual disciplines. Be innovative and inquisitive in your pursuit of knowledge. Be willing to read new books and explore new thoughts! Try fasting for three days and nights. Spend a week without talking. Embark on a vision quest to a secluded location. Spend a year studying the Song of Songs. Learn a new language. Challenge the familiar. Tear up your old maps (the ones with boundaries). Chart new terrain in the name of Jesus. Look at the ocean of ministry; it is so expansive. Venture out onto the open sea!

> *Adventure with God. Journey with Him in the wild terrain. Breathe in the fresh air. Chase after the Poem that can only be heard outside the confines of the castle gate.*

Advancing From Talk to Walk

The mindset of advancement must give birth to structural change. A proper foundation is essential if your church is to be a force for the Kingdom. God has a divine design for the community of faith. Decide right now that you will not settle for second best. You are going to have to clear the rubble field and dig deep in order to do the foundational work. When you start making adjustments on a foundational level, the whole building will be shaken. God shakes everything. He wants you to see what will fall out and what sticks.

Of course, not everything is up for grabs. The principles of Scriptures are unchanging as is God's character. The mission of the church — to continue the work that Jesus began in His earthly ministry through the power of His Spirit — may change in form, but not in its ultimate goal of salvation and justice for all.

Our faith contains a healthy tension between that which is to never change and that which must change. As Eugene Peterson states, "We want a Christian faith that has stability but is not petrified; [one] that has vision but is not hallucinatory."[31] Be discerning in this regard as you move forward as a church community.

Establish right priorities: His Kingdom, His culture, His way, and His will—not ours. Establish proper alignment: God first, Kingdom work first. Feelings and comfort need to be way down on the list if they figure into to it at all. Right structures need to be set in place.

As mentioned previously, we advance on our knees. We move forward on our faces. The fiercest battle takes place in the realm of intercession. Prayer covering is vital. Advancement begins when a pastor chooses to be unashamedly devoted to meeting with God. Intimacy with God and desperation for a move of God are the pre-requisites for change. Pastor, once your lifestyle is aligned with the will of God in this regard, begin building an army of intercessors. Intercession is foolishness to the world. Pray for such foolishness in your church. Pray for tenaciously foolish people who will stand with you and your leadership on the front lines of battle.

Advancing Into the New

Do not be afraid to call forth new wineskins within your church. Just because a committee or a procedure has been around for a long time does not make it untouchable. Look at the ground. Is it fallow? If so, work the soil of your ministry. Otherwise, it will be fruitless.

Imagine a farmer working diligently in his fields. From dawn until dusk, he labors to produce a harvest. But instead of planting seed, he's planting grains of sand. This is fruitless work. All his labor, all his investment of time and energy, all the water and nutrients will amount to nothing. He cannot produce a harvest from a grain of sand. He needs good seed.

What's the good seed?
Nothing but Jesus!
Nothing but the fire!
Nothing but radical discipleship!
Nothing but Acts 2 leading to Matthew 28!

Seek after the Presence of God. Chase after and then remain in His Presence. Strength, inspiration, courage, joy, anointing—all flow from being in His

Presence. Without the pillar of fire, the Tabernacle is nothing more than a tent. Without the Presence of God, our worship services are nothing more than empty religion. Plant seed, not sand.

Beware of fruitless vines. They look so healthy! They expand over great areas, taking nutrients of the church to feed themselves, yet they produce no fruit. Don't hesitate to take the ax and cut them off at the root.

Beware of fruitless meetings: Doing the same things the same way does not make sense if no eternal fruit comes from it. Are your committee meetings resulting in more harm than good? Break up the fallow ground, turn the weeds over and refresh the soil.

> *Without the pillar of fire, the Tabernacle is nothing more than a tent.*

If the pillar of fire is not over the Tent of Meeting, pray and pray and fast and pray until the fire appears—because apart from the Presence of God, the church is powerless and lost.

Beware of fruitlessness!

Beware of fruitless words. Words that are repeated again and again yet produce no eternal fruit need to be eliminated from your vocabulary.

Beware of fruitless associations, partnerships and friendships. The Spirit of God wants to plant an orchard in your life for His glory. Don't fill up the acreage with fruitless endeavors.

Clear the field! After fasting and praying, after getting clear direction from the Lord, clear the land! Do the hard work. Bring out the chain saw and the stump grinder. Pile up all the dead branches on the side of the field. Clear the rubble out of the way. Then bring in the plow. Be careful to plant good seed. God will be faithful and cause the growth.

One more word about change: Be thankful if your church is in transition and being stretched. The most frightening prospect is the church that has become dormant and is dying a slow, cold death. Keep the fires burning! Teach about change. Introduce variations in the worship and prayer times. Find times to talk about new experiences. In this way, you are inoculating your congregation against becoming the "frozen chosen."

I agree with Leith Anderson when he states: "As soon as people walk into a church, they can tell if it is oriented toward the past or the future."[32] Glance at the past, but focus on the future. Let people see the unfolding vision of the Kingdom of God advancing in your community.

Advancing Beyond Our Walls

You are called to a shepherding ministry in your local church under the direction of the Chief Shepherd. He is concerned not only about those in your church, but also about "Jerusalem, Judea, Samaria and the ends of the earth" (Acts 1:8). The two spheres must connect. Inside the walls must get outside the walls. If you work only within the church, your ministry will not flourish under God's greater blessing.

A few years ago, I believe the Lord gave me the following picture:

I envisioned a field being farmed. A small portion of the field was being fertilized and watered—it was like a garden. The larger portion of the field was ignored.

Even though there were many workers in the small garden, it seemed as if they were laboring in vain. Ten people were gathered around two or three plants, not just for a few minutes, but for days at a time. I continued to watch the work of these people even though I was disturbed by what I saw.

The Lord asked me to lift up my eyes and look around. I looked up and saw the expanse of land surrounding this small garden plot. There were acres and acres of farmland, most of it uncultivated. From this new perspective, the work in the garden seemed strangely ingrown and myopic.

I asked one of the workers why this small garden was receiving so much attention when the fields surrounding it were receiving none. He answered, "Every time we pass by this plot, the plants scream and cry out for more food, water and attention. They seem so full of pain and misery that all of us become deeply concerned for their welfare. We work to quench their thirst and desire to see them grow. Before long, the sun is setting and we realize that we've spent another full day in the garden."

"Does this garden seem to benefit from all your labor?" I asked.

"That's the strangest thing," the other said. "With all this attention, one would think that this garden would be flourishing. But I'm beginning to think that

all our support is making these plants weaker rather than stronger."

"What about these other fields?" I asked. "Are they not also the property of the One who owns the garden?"

"Yes, and we are certain He wants us to farm that land also. But if we are unable to cause this little garden to grow, how can we move on to a more expansive mission?"

Our conversation ended abruptly as the Owner Himself walked towards us. He had chosen this day to inspect the work in His fields. He came to the crowded garden area, knelt down and tenderly touched each emaciated plant.

"These plants must choose whether or not they want to flourish," He said. "They have grown dependent upon all your service and have not yet been given an opportunity to decide for themselves whether or not they want to enter into the work of living and producing fruit for others. You do well to continue caring for them, but only to the extent that you care for the rest of the field."

Then I watched the Owner stand up and look at the fields around Him. His eyes moved across the acres of land that had remained untouched in this season. The farm workers and I naturally began to look where He was looking, and we began to see what He was seeing.

All of this land: uncultivated, untouched, uncared for.

The Owner was silent as he gazed over the fields. The waiting was uncomfortable. Then His gaze fell upon us.

"How has this happened?" He asked. "How is it that these fields have received nothing from your hand? Was it not clear that I placed all of these fields under your supervision?"

The workers nodded. The Owner called them to come closer. He laid His hands on the shoulders of the ones nearest Him. Tenderly, yet sternly, He said, "My friends, what I require of you is obedience to My commands. The growth of the plants and the size of the harvest are in many ways beyond your control, but your obedience is not. There are many voices telling you to 'Come here' and 'Do this,' but it is My voice you must obey. Pledge to Me now that you will faithfully work in all the fields that I have set before you. And when I return for My next inspection, I will be able to say, 'Well done, good and faithful servant!'"

The workers pledged their commitment anew, and so did I.

It is not comfortable to lift our eyes and see all of the fields we have not cultivated. It is not easy to watch the Master's eyes as he looks over the neighborhoods, the schools, the streets, the towns that He has placed under our supervision, but this is the first incision of His scalpel into our callused hearts. It is our awakening to look beyond our small garden.

Many pastors are not comfortable in their own skin. We are taught to relate to people from behind the pulpit or through a liturgy, and so some of us simply don't know how to "be" with people. There are dozens of books on evangelism and wonderful teaching and conferences on the topic, yet I can count on one hand the pastors I actually see walking the streets and practicing evangelism.

Do you want to learn? Are you willing to be a beginner? This new mindset will require courage. The journey to the fields is less about technique and more about stepping out of one's comfort zone.

How do you make this transition? Leave the church building! Get out before it's too late! The administration, the background noise of the organization, the appointments, the study—it's all part of a pastor's call, but it will claim every last drop of our blood if we're not careful. Don't wait for a quiet day. If we wait for things to settle down in our congregations, we might as well abandon all hope of ever making it to the fields. The time has come to be proactive. Schedule part of every day (even if it's thirty minutes) for "field" work. Explore! Let me state it again: God is a pioneer and He wants us to join Him in His adventure of reaching the lost and mending what has been broken.

Go to the streets of your town. Sit down on a bench. Ask the Lord for His vision for the acres and acres of uncultivated land. If you ask Him, He will give you opportunities to stretch. Make it a goal to enter into a conversation with someone you have never met. There are millions of "strangers" in the world. Once you learn to break through the "stranger

> *Leave the church building! Administration is part of a pastor's call—but it will claim every last drop of our blood if we're not careful.*

barrier," a whole new terrain of ministry is available to you!

Thankfully, the church sends missionaries all over the world. Each missionary must learn the language, customs and culture of the people they are trying to reach with the gospel. It is necessary to become a student of the culture in order to reach the culture. How precious is the missionary who learns to speak French in order to be taught Wolof! How beautiful is the commitment of the missionary who studies Spanish for five years in order to effectively reach those in Ecuador.

Who is studying the stranger barrier? Who are the missionaries to the thousands of people all around us who are not being reached with the gospel? Decide today to learn how to cross over that stranger barrier and work outside the garden gate.

Our daily schedules are an outward manifestation of an inward work. The primary work is the shift in the core of our beings. We must determine within ourselves that we will no longer pastor garden churches. Most churches cater to long-time believers and compete for the Christian market. Most church growth in the West is not about new conversions to Christ. Rather, churches are growing primarily from digging up plants and moving them to another row in the garden.

There are thousands of "garden variety" churches already. Why not journey into the fields? There are acres and acres of uncultivated fields. Choose to be one of the pastors who actually get out of the garden.

People who are self-absorbed and who only receive will never be healthy. We are created in the image of God and therefore are created to receive *and* give. A dammed up river becomes a cesspool.

There is a difference between being a "garden" prophet and a "field" prophet. A garden prophet gives pictures about people in the church feeling alone and unloved. These pictures and words are all about comforting the comfortable and feeding those who just don't like what's on the menu. Is this a valid ministry? Well, yes and no. Yes, there are wounds in the church and God cares about every person. No, God does not desire us to focus on ourselves 24/7/365 for eighty years and then die.

A field prophet submits a challenging word outside the status quo, a raised voice in the midst of the uncultivated terrain. God wants us to be light and salt. He wants us to live in such a way that people see the power of God and know that Jesus is alive and that He cares.

Advancing the Poor and Marginalized

One Sunday, a visitor came to our church and introduced himself as an evangelist who lived a distance away. He was simply joining us for the service that morning. At the break, I entered into a conversation with him. He told me that when he enters a town, he visits the homeless shelters, inquires what churches minister to that population, and then attends one of those churches the following Sunday.

Do they mention the name of our churches in the shelters? If not, we must make changes so that a year from now they will. There are people who live within blocks of our churches who are marginalized. God is calling us to minister to the poor and disenfranchised. Every church is called to feed the hungry, visit those in prison, pray for the sick and proclaim justice for all.

Pastor, do not become paralyzed by the scope of this mission. Rather, be stirred by it. Start with one consistent outreach: a monthly service at the county prison, serving a meal at the local shelter, or starting a small food pantry for the community. The simple act of serving others will begin to change hearts within your church community.

It is important that you personally give yourself to this work (especially at first), but you will be surprised how such practice becomes contagious. Others will begin to see what you are doing and catch on to God's heartbeat for the broken and tormented. Soon you will begin to see a population within your church catching fire with the vision of service and outreach.

By building relationships with people who have been marginalized by society in some way, those who are not marginalized will become more aware of their own hypocrisy and game-playing. As Paul Goodman writes, "[The poor] don't let you be phony with them. They live closer to reality—to death and life and despair and hope. The poor have less to hide behind. There is no cushion of money and things to help them appear to themselves and to others what they are not, and they don't have people holding them to acceptable patterns of behavior."[33]

The establishment of practical ministry that addresses the brokenness in your own neighborhood will bring a stirring of life into your church. It is interesting isn't it? Something so central to the biblical message has become so foreign to our daily lives. The modern day church struggles to see the desperate souls who sit at the foot of the gaudy, neon signs of our self-absorbed lives.

Advancing to the Ends of the Earth

Even though there are many people to be evangelized in your own town, continue to extend to the nations. We must teach our congregations that God's mission is bigger than us and bigger than our culture.

Church communities change locally as prayers for countries like Burma, Bhutan, and Cambodia are lifted up within our sanctuaries. As we pray for the world—for those imprisoned in China, for the millions of children around the world who are forced into the worse kind of slavery, for the 200 million Christians who are harassed, abused, tortured and martyred simply because of their faith in Jesus — the biblical revelation that God loves the world becomes a tangible reality not just a theological premise.

Go to the nations (start with short term mission trips), and bring the nations to your church (invite pastors from other countries and those who have been persecuted for their faith to come and preach on a Sunday morning). When you both go and bring, you are sowing Kingdom seeds into your church's field of vision. As you move in this way, minds will open, hearts will break and souls will light on fire. Teach about the 10-40 window. Inform your congregation about unreached people groups. Pray for economic justice and fair trade (and live in congruence with your prayers). Raise funds for the drilling of a new well in a village in Africa.

American Christians are insulated from the rawness of trying to survive daily on less than a dollar a day. Books, videos and education help in the uncomfortable process of having our eyes opened to the brokenness of the world. Inviting a speaker who has first-hand experience is even more revealing. Actually witnessing it first-hand is the best. The sights, the smells, the tastes of another culture will change a person's worldview more rapidly than anything else. Such learning is invaluable and should be pursued.

In many churches, there is a conflict between infrastructure and outreach. Some people cry out for more of the church budget to be allocated to global mission. Others cry out for the home front to be the top priority. As pastor, you must teach that both are important. Teach about the "storehouse of the Lord." Promote tithing into the storehouse so that when the Lord calls

> *Teach our congregations that God's mission is bigger than us and bigger than our culture.*

the church to send a missionary or purchase another building, you are able to move in His timing. At a minimum, allocate 10% of your general budget for mission work outside the walls of your church. Increase this as the Lord blesses.

Moving Forward

A church that is not sending missionaries is not a mature church. Pastor, promote the cause of those who have little or nothing. Awaken the compassion of the Lord within the hearts of your congregants. You are called to be a leader in the cause of missions! Teach, preach, equip and go to the nations. The Lord will bless every pastor who does such things with zealous and joyous co-workers who have caught the vision of the Kingdom!

Epilogue
Remember the Joy
of the Lord

J oy, which was the small publicity of the pagan, is
the gigantic secret of the Christian.
— G.K. Chesterton

The Bible says, "Do not grieve, for the joy of the
Lord is your strength" (Neh.8:10). I have found this
to be true: Without God's joy, I would be overcome
by fear, anxiety and responsibility. The task is too
great and the burden is too heavy for me in my own
strength. God, however, has a secret weapon for us:
He wants to fill us up with His joy!

It was the joy of the Lord that caused Ignatius, in
the year A.D.110, to appeal to the Church of Rome
not to try to deliver him from martyrdom "because
they would deprive him of that which he most longed
and hoped for."[34] It was the joy of the Lord that
caused Perpetua to see her dungeon as a palace. [35]
It was the same infilling that caused Cyril, "the 84-

year old bishop of the church at Gortyna to display no fear when Lucius condemned him to be burned at the stake, and [he] suffered the flames joyously and with great courage." [36]

Pastor Richard Wurmbrand writes: "When I look back on my fourteen years in prison, it was occasionally a very happy time. Other prisoners and even the guards very often wondered at how happy Christians could be under the most terrible circumstances." [37]

Not many of us have had to endure such hardship, yet many believers live defeated and joyless lives. Some pastors are so heavy-laden they can barely walk. It seems like they haven't laughed in a decade. With faces contorted and backs bent, they move through their day as if the weight of the whole world is on their shoulders.

Certainly the pressure is real. The ministry, at times, can be overwhelming, but God doesn't want His shepherds walking around like they are barely in the ranks of the living. He wants to shock the world by shining His joy through our broken lives.

Recently, the Lord showed me that I had lost my childlikeness. In a very gentle way, He revealed the fact that years before, I smiled and laughed more. The cares of the world, my compassion for hurting people, the intensity of ministry—all had become a heavy yoke upon my shoulders. The Lord was showing me that He was delighted that I cared so deeply for people, but that my testimony was not complete without His joy pouring through me. I began crying out for an anointing of joy, peace and power in my life and ministry. I asked God to deliver me from looping thoughts that were leading me around the same mountain and filling me with heaviness and despair.

I am actively cooperating with the Lord concerning the renewing of my mind; I don't want discouraging and frustrating thoughts to steal away my testimony of joy in this broken and frenetic world.

The world is searching for joy, yet apart from Christ, all that can be found is a temporary diversion. Eugene Peterson describes the enormous entertainment industry in America as a court jester employed by our society to divert its attention after an over-indulgent meal.[38] God's intention is that, when our neighbors look at us, they will see a deeper, more permanent joy springing up in our lives.

Karl Barth, author of a six-million word, twelve-volume work on dogmatics (plus forty or fifty other books), wrote: "The theologian who has no joy in his work is not a theologian at all. Sulky faces, morose thoughts and boring ways of speaking are intolerable in this science."

> *We must learn the secret that has been the battle cry of millions of believers throughout history: "The joy of the Lord is my strength!"*

We must learn the secret that has been the battle cry of millions of believers throughout history: "The joy of the Lord is my strength!" When circumstances press in on you, remember who lives inside of you and rejoice! When you are weary because of the burden on your shoulders, remember who lives inside of you and rejoice. When you are placed in the fiery furnace and, in the natural, there doesn't seem to be a way of escape, remember who walks with you and rejoice.

God's joy has miracle working power. Grab onto it and don't let it go. In His strength we can do amazing things!

Final Word and Blessing

Pastor, thank you for your ministry to the Body of Christ and for your witness to the world! My prayer is that you have been strengthened and encouraged by the words in this book. If you have received any helpful insights, inspiration or refreshment from these pages, I am honored and blessed to have served you in the name of our Lord Jesus Christ. This is our time to shine. We are on this earth for only a moment and have been blessed with a great commissioning. We have been given a great gospel to proclaim and are empowered with the Holy Spirit.

I am praying that you stand your post and don't back away. I pray that the joy of the Lord will be your strength and that Jesus Himself will give you wisdom to equip and prepare your congregation for works of service and Kingdom advancement. Continue standing, continue running, and continue dreaming!

"To him who is able to keep you from falling and to present you before his glorious presence without fault and with great joy—to the only God our Savior be glory, majesty, power and authority, through Jesus Christ our Lord, before all ages, now and forever-more" (Jude 24-25)!

Amen.

Appendix 1: A Survival Kit for the Desert

Build this kit (in the form of a file, a box, or what-ever works for you) immediately; continue to add to it and have it within reach always.

A Confidant: Include the name of at least one confidant outside your church system. Have his/her phone number in your survival kit. This means the person understands his/her mission and has given you permission to call at any time. The relationship must be developed and maintained so that when you find yourself in the desert without many options, this can be a lifeline.

A Retreat Option: Have an agreement with your elders or your bishop—that if things get very intense, you have permission to request three or four days away without having to "sell" the idea to them. You are more than willing to offer an explanation after your retreat. Do not use this option unless you are truly in the desert. Have a place already arranged— not too far (but far enough), not too expensive (but have money saved for the occasion).

A Declaration Paper: Include a declaration paper in your survival kit—a list of declarations that speak to your identity and destiny. These affirmations are written in the good times so that when all is crashing around you and you find yourself in the desert place, the words will provide an oasis of protection from the deep arrows of the enemy.

Two or Three Important Letters from friends and parishioners: include in your survival kit a few letters/e-mails that bless you in a special way and that confirm your call.

Prophetic Pictures that have been confirmed and **Life Verses** from the Bible. Have these handy—written out and in a file labeled "Desert Survival Kit."

Procedural Commitments: Write down how you will make decisions while in the desert and do not give yourself to your feelings in the season. Examples:

*I will pray before acting
*I will seek counsel from 2-3 different sources
*I will not act independently. I will walk in community.
*I will fast
*I will wait upon the Lord and be careful to hear what He's saying to me
*I will journal

Gather this survival kit and know where it is at all times. Continue to add to it as the Lord gives you wisdom. Believe me, this will be a welcome friend numerous times in your ministry career.

Appendix 2: Paradigm shifts in my Pastoral Ministry

Every once in a while, a new thought stirs our imaginations and begins to challenge some of our deepest and most long-standing foundational understandings of life. These revelations are tremendous gifts and can produce shifts and quantum leaps in faith and ministry. These are some of my major discoveries as a pastor over the past eighteen years. Please note that I am being purposeful in my lack of detail, as I would encourage you to meditate upon them yourself, allowing them to grow in you.

Organization vs. Organism

Within most organizations, a worker can't just walk into the CEO's office. Within an organism, parts of the body are connected directly to the head through the neurological system. Jesus is the Head of the Church. Every saint is directly connected to Him. The church is not primarily a human institution but a living organism (the Body of Christ). This idea of *organism* opens up important relational truths about the church; all organisms must be nourished, fight off sickness, eliminate toxins, reproduce in order to survive, etc.

Consensus doesn't always mean 100% agreement.

Decision-making is a very important aspect of church life. Who makes directional decisions for your church, and what process is followed?

Consensus among an elder team is the best option. It may seem that waiting for every elder to agree on a path forward is cumbersome and lethargic. However, I have witnessed occasions when one person disagreed with the group, and through prayer and discussion, the whole group shifted because of the one person's perspective. In order for consensus to work among an elder team:

[1] Each leader must release personal agendas, desiring only God's will for the church.
[2] Each elder must be willing to listen to other perspectives and not close off from other ways of thinking.
[3] A broad understanding of consensus must be consistently taught and modeled.

Consensus does not mean that everyone agrees with every detail of a proposal, but the general direction can be agreed upon. There is a difference between a "concern" and a "check" in moving forward. This distinction is vital to consider and develop.

Servant leadership can be strong leadership.

The teachings of Jesus challenge many secular presuppositions about leadership and servanthood. Our common understanding is that a leader has power and value; a servant has neither. A leader is "over" and a servant is "under;" being a leader is honorable and being a servant is undignified.

Jesus breaks open our paradigms of leadership by connecting these two seemingly incongruent characteristics. He calls church leaders to be humble, empowering servants, but does not desire them to abdicate their role to lead with strength. This line of thinking is worthy of much study and meditation.

The Broad Theological Theme of Reconciliation

Consider the Bible as separated into three main sections:

[1] Genesis 1-2 — God's intention for creation before sin entered the cosmos
[2] Genesis 3-Matthew 1 — the brokenness of creation due to the fall of Adam and Eve
[3] Matthew 1-Revelation 22 — the redemptive work of Christ, who came to restore what was broken.

God did not intend brokenness. Sin entered through one act of disobedience. It was like a pebble thrown into a calm pond and creating ripples. Unlike a natural pond, these ripples increased the further removed they were from the source. Sin and brokenness increased through time up until the event of the cross. What had become a tsunami wave struck the cross — and went no further. In fact, the wave reversed its course and became a work of redemption, taking back ground for the Kingdom of God.

What is our Lord doing every day? He is working for reconciliation. Where there is loneliness, the Spirit longs to bring *koinonia* connection. Where there is hopelessness, He desires to bring hope. This is true in all realms of brokenness — broken bodies, broken minds, broken relationships, broken economic systems, and more. God is always working for reconciliation and restoration. Jesus calls His church to join Him in this mission.

Do not quench the Spirit's fire.

I read 1 Thessalonians 5:19 hundreds of times before I actually started to think about how to put such an admonition into practice in my personal, family and pastoral life. The shift of thinking was this: *Quenching the Spirit's fire is a serious sin.* When we quench the Spirit, we are working against our Lord's purposes. While He is working towards reconciliation and revival, we are trying to slow the progress.

Do I really want the fire? Am I courageous enough to say, "Lord, whatever You are doing, I will fan the flame"? A shift will occur in life and in the church as we begin to put this verse into practice. Meanwhile, it challenges comfort zones beyond imagination!

The Radical Middle

For years, my thinking about the term *radical* moved in linear progression. Now I believe that the most radical (severely difficult but God-ordained) position of the church can be best described with the phrase "the radical middle." Bill Jackson speaks of this interesting distinction in this book, *The Quest for the Radical Middle*:

> Satan's strategy, as we have hypothesized,
> is to pull a person, church or movement

away from the radical middle toward one pole or the other. In this case he pits Word against Spirit, reason against experience, organization against organism. Church movements are fluid, starting on the Spirit side of the continuum as people crave experiential reality. Then they move toward the Word side as they seek to ground their experience in biblical objectivity.[39]

High tension	Experiential	The	Reasoned	Low Tension
Weird	Spontaneous	Radical	Organized	Dead
Cultism	Heart	Middle	Head	Orthodoxy

Hold to the Word of God *and* allow the Holy Spirit freedom to move. It is both/and, not either/or. Do not give any ground. Too far to the right or left is "missing the mark" for normative, biblical Christianity.

From Ruts to Exit Ramps

All people, including pastors, can wake up one day and find themselves in a rut, wondering how long they have been there. Recognizing that fact is a big step in recovery, so how about you? Take assessment of your life. Are you stuck in your thought patterns, in an attitude, in a behavior, in your schedule, in your eating, in a relationship, in your ministry context?

It's time for heavy construction: build an exit ramp! This sounds exciting at first (and it is). But such road work will make a mess and create a traffic jam in the rut. Not everyone will be excited about the changes. Still, resolve to push through because you must! Create that exit ramp! Otherwise, you will continue going around the same mountain forever!

I cannot imagine Jesus ever being caught in a rut. The Lord does not intend for any of His people to be enslaved to such mindsets. Develop a distaste for ruts, hone your eyesight to spot them more quickly, then build an exit ramp in the name of Jesus and start living in a new way!

From Closed Boxes to Open Lids

Boxes are limiting structures and the adversaries of vision and change. Without realizing it, we can confine the work of the Lord into them. Reductive or minimizing language and behavior are dishonoring to Him and quench His Spirit. Doubting God's power to heal dishonors Him. Questioning God's ability to intervene proclaims Him to be smaller and less powerful than He really is. God can make dead bones live (Ezek.37:3)! He created the universe out of nothing! He can bring forth beauty from ashes!

Make it your goal to never box God in—not in your theology, or your preaching, or your prayers. Are you disturbed when someone uses the Name of Jesus as a curse word? Be equally disturbed at any portrayal of the Living God as weak and powerless!

Box language is old, expected and lifeless. Vision language is new, surprising and bursting with vitality. Box language speaks in "realistic" terms. Vision language entertains the impossible. Box thinking is defeated by a lid. Vision thinking is not intimidated by a lid.

In the Name of Christ, find the boxes in your thinking and in your church, and then wage war against them. To join Him in this work, you must begin to think in terms of *can* rather than *can't*. These are huge shifts in the mind of a pastor. I agree with Bill Hybels when he calls vision "a leader's most potent weapon.[9]" Become fluent in the language of biblical faith and vision. Then, speak it and preach it and live it out in front of your congregation.

From Acorns to Oak Trees

Value and celebrate small beginnings. Kingdom work almost always starts small and unseen. The mustard seed, the yeast, the manger—God's revolution begins in the hidden places, but has great potential to bring forth change.

I once heard of a man who, while holding an acorn, said, "Look at the mighty oak tree in my hand." God sees our potential and speaks to our prophetic destiny. Look at the acorn and "do not despise the day of small beginnings" (Zech.4:10).

Presently, your congregation may be small or large in number. Remember this: the size, the symmetry and shape of the acorn really aren't important. It is what you *do* with that acorn. Will you place it in good soil? Will you provide fresh water and good nutrients? Give no thought for appearances; what you see now must change anyway.

Many pastors spend years polishing an acorn. "Look at our church—the shiniest acorn in the county!" But the acorn needs to fall to the ground and die in order for something greater to be birthed. Stop polishing what you have. Look forward to what God will do through His miracle of transformation. Be faithful in the administration of your ministry and do not despise the day of small beginnings.

In a sense, it doesn't matter where you start. If the man with ten talents buried all of his Master's money in the ground, then he would have been the one who was rebuked. If the man with one talent invested his Master's money wisely, then he would have received the blessing. No matter what you have in the present moment, reframe your perspective and establish a mustard seed mentality. Catch God's prophetic dream for your ministry. The key is not to look with our natural eyes, but with the eyes of faith.

This is a simple idea. But it is difficult to keep your thinking squarely on this truth. Everywhere and all the time, people are assessing success with natural eyes. There is a lot of acorn polishing going on around us and inside of us. The Lord is asking us to follow His example: to release our hands and allow the acorn drop to the ground. All the time and energy that has committed to protecting and grooming the acorn can be reallocated to a new way of living.

Appendix 3: Surviving Spiritual Revival

It may seem strange to see the words survival and revival in the same sentence, but be certain of this: Wherever and whenever God is on the move, the enemy steps up his attack.

Do you long to see revival in your church? This is certainly God's heart for every local assembly, but make sure you count the cost of revival before you proceed. Every spiritual awakening in history has gotten messy and people have left the church. If the Spirit of God brings revival to your church, your experience will be no different.

Here's what I have learned about revival in the church:

God loves the desperate prayers of His people.

He loves people to seek His face and want more of Him. Be steadfast in corporate prayer; spend hours crying out to God, asking Him to reveal Himself and to further His Kingdom through your assembly. Spend hours repenting for quenching His Spirit, for being afraid, for controlling worship services and not giving the Lord freedom to move however He wants. Offer times of confession, repentance, adoration, worship and praise.

Along with your weekly prayer meetings, initiate monthly vigils (prayer times of at least five hours in duration). God is moving in many areas of the world today, especially in Africa. The leaders of these movements point to the prayer vigils as a key ingredient in cooperating with the Lord in His work.

The seeds of revival are the desperate prayers of the saints (vigils are revival sowing times). The water of revival is the willingness of the people of God to wait upon the Lord as their only hope for transformation (vigils are soaking times, hours of waiting and wrestling in the Spirit). The springing up of revival occurs when people become solely committed to living a Spirit-filled life in obedience to God's Word (and vigils press a congregation toward a radicalized commitment to biblical discipleship).

Add fasting to your prayers.

Invite your entire congregation to join you and your leadership in scheduled fasts. This discipline opens eyes, ears and hearts to the work God is already doing.

Be strategic in your scheduling of fasts, aligning them with the prayer vigils, special anniversaries, prophetic moments, intensive battles, starting lines, etc. Fasting and prayer operating together are forceful weapons in the spiritual battle, but because of the self-denial inherent in these disciplines, only a small percentage of churches practice them consistently.

Do you want to see your community transformed? Do you long to see your church on fire to fulfill the Great Commission? No revival in history has arisen apart from prayer and fasting.

Work with your leadership first before you move in the congregation.

It is vital that you prepare your leaders for survival in revival, as they will be in for the battle of their lives. Give them books to read concerning the great revivals of church history. Work hard to develop the team's ability to discern truth from falsehood and to distinguish the works of the Holy Spirit from counterfeit manifestations. Practice a team mentality in ministry times; learn how to work together! God will use all of you to confirm the activity of the Spirit and to provide protection for the church when it is needed.

Explain to your leaders that everyone's comfort zone will be invaded when God begins to move in a congregation. Everyone will be stretched. There will be some wonderful breakthroughs and some stunning set-backs. Just as an emergency room physician must set the broken bone in spite of the patient's discomfort, so too, your leadership team must not back away as the Chief Physician properly sets the broken bones in His Body. Revival alignment is radical and costly. For God's reign to manifest more fully, a local church must shift from "normal for us" to "normal in the Bible." The Word of God challenges the status quo entitlements of comfort, convenience and control. This message is one of discipleship: denying self, taking up our crosses and following Jesus. This is not popular, but it is biblical.

The enemy will try to divide your leaders, so prepare them for the onslaught. Make sure your leadership is with you and fully committed before you begin praying for revival, because there will be a strong temptation to turn back once difficulty begins.

Teach your congregation to focus on the Lord and not on manifestations.

We know that God works in mysterious ways; indeed, this is the teaching of the Bible. Naaman was asked to dip himself in the Jordan River seven times, Joshua was told to march with a praise band around the walls of Jericho, and Jesus placed mud on the eyes of the blind man. God never moves in a way that contradicts the principles of His Word, but He often moves in ways that stretch us beyond our religious comfort zones.

If we long for revival in our churches, we must allow the Holy Spirit room to move. As people are touched by Him, manifestations (falling down in prayer, shaking, emotional stirrings, new gifts, new revelation, etc) may occur. Explain this to your congregation. Take time to look at various Scriptures where people fall down before the Lord "as dead." When the Almighty God touches a human heart, what should we expect?

My conclusion is that there are many possibilities—outward manifestations or no manifestations at all, lots of emotion or no emotion at all, a sense of closeness to the Lord or no sense at all. Choose not to focus on what's happening in people. Rather, choose to focus on the Lord moving among His people. Be thankful for miracles, but also *glory* in the Presence of the Living God. Praise God for healings, miracles, deliverances and prophetic words delivered to the heart, yet all else pales in comparison to the wonder and glory of the King of Kings walking among His people. Focus on Him!

You and those you appoint must lead during ministry times. Your mission is two-fold:

[1] to protect the flock (not allowing anything but the kerygma[41] to be taught, no name but Jesus to be glorified and no gospel to be preached but the one proclaimed in the New Testament)

[2] to minister to the flock by allowing the Holy Spirit freedom to move.

You must be absolutely resolved on these two tasks.

Everyone has a part to play in corporate worship services, but as pastor, your role is unique. Your congregation must come to trust your intentions and your competence to intervene in order to provide protection and advancement. They must come to believe that you have the courage to stop an activity that is out of order and also the courage to allow manifestations that you sense are from the Lord.

I am not speaking of a blind trust. The congregation must understand that you and your leaders will not be perfect in your gate-keeping, and that there will be a need for correction from time to time. Some people will not accept anything but mistake-free discernment. Such people will struggle to remain in a community that believes in the supernatural interventions of the Spirit of God. Others will see your heart and, after observing your consistency, will stand with you. Be sure to offer explanation in the midst of confusion and correction when you've missed something. This is all part of the journey of trust-building for your church.

Invite guest speakers.

Healthy church life includes inviting gifted ministers from outside your community to share vision and preach the Word. Such practice is especially strategic in times of revival. When you do so, prepare your congregation by explaining that no vessel is perfect. There will be edges in every prophet, evangelist and conference speaker. No one is without human frailty. Urge your congregation to extend grace to one another and to those entering your church.

Assure your people that you and the elders will provide watchcare and will not allow false teaching or false ministry to enter the church. At the same time, explain to them that you will not be correcting the punctuation of a person's delivery (minor infractions are handled differently than major ones). Teach your congregation not to quench the Holy Spirit but to test all things by the Word of God. Exhort them to be humble, wise, and gracious. Teach them to eat what is good and spit out what is not.

It is essential that your congregation develop both the tenacity and the noble character of the Bereans (Acts 17:11-12). A mature church has both of their traits: a resolute conviction to hold to the Word of God and noble character with a willingness to listen graciously and be stretched. Promote such things!

Bless people as they leave your church.

Revival brings about change. Change produces fear and unrest in many people. Some will resign their membership and leave. Your ministry may be spoken of as unbalanced or even false and dangerous.

Do not become defensive. Do not try to validate yourself. Take courage! These shifts within the congregation are a necessary stage in God's redemptive work. Pray that every person staying in your church will be more invested than they were before in the vision of God's work. Pray that every person who leaves will find another church where they can serve Him effectively. Listen carefully to the people's complaints as the leave the church. Test and examine all things to ensure that you are not moving away from Scriptural principles. If you are within the Word of God, don't turn back.

Throughout these fiery ordeals, walk in holiness and integrity. Holiness is a glorious and vicious weapon against Satan and his demonic powers. It is like a trumpet announcing the emergence of the Kingdom of God and the eventual destruction of the kingdom of this world.

Maintain your integrity. Always take the high road. Give the enemy no ammunition. Don't worry about your reputation. Don't be concerned about the falsehoods spoken about you; but be very concerned about living and ministering with integrity at all times. In the end, you'll be able look everyone squarely in the eye and sleep soundly at night.

Be thankful for brothers and sisters who co-labor with you in church ministry. Every person who ministers faithfully beside you is a blessing from God. But do not believe, even for a moment, that this or that person is so foundational to the work that if they left, the work would crumble. Everyone is valuable to the work (if they are fully committed to God's purposes), but the survival of the church depends on only One person: Jesus, the ever-reigning Lord!

It is a tough day when faithful co-workers inform you that they are stepping away from your ministry team. It's a tough day, but it's not the end of the world. The God who can cause "stones to cry out" His praises (Lk.19:40) can most certainly bring new workers into your church.

Expect aftershocks.

During revival, keep focused on the vision. If you try to keep track of people coming and going, your head will swivel so much you'll need a neck brace. You will be surprised at how many new people show up; there are people whose hearts are burning for the manifest Presence of God and won't settle for anything less.

There will come a time when the nucleus of your community will seem to stabilize. Don't relax completely; usually there are aftershocks that follow the major earthquake. Revival will rock you to the core and your church to its very foundations. Many people have prayed for revival, but then, when the Holy Spirit shows up, they start praying for His departure.

If you truly surrender to the Lord, what a beautifully anticipated moment it will be when the birth pangs of revival begin among your people. The labor pains and will be intense, but a new church will be born. When it's all said and done, perhaps more than half of your members will leave. Don't be discouraged. Hundreds of others will come, and they will be just as hungry as you are for more of God!

Appendix 4: The Identity School for Christian Ministry

If you are interested in further study concerning surviving and thriving in ministry, I invite you to consider enrolling in the Identity School for Christian Ministry (www.theidentityschool.com). The key survival tools outlined in this book are taught in an experiential learning format through the following course:

Survival Ministry Training (MST-101) — This course covers five practical and essential keys for survival.

Module #1: Know Yourself — Each student is guided through discovery of [1] his/her own blind spots and triggers and [2] how to respond by the Spirit of God.

Module #2: Know Your Enemy — Students become [1] aware of the spiritual strategies of the adversary toward pastors and missionaries and [2] proficient in biblical techniques of spiritual warfare.

Module #3: Assess the Terrain — Students [1] become aware of the relational dynamics within their systems of ministry and [2] develop strategies and structures that bring life and health to these systems.

Module #4: Know Your God — Students learn [1] to articulate and reaffirm God's love and calling on their lives and [2] to establish life structures that promote God's Word and Spirit to be the primary influences on their identity and calling.

Module #5: Know Your Mission — Students [1] learn to articulate their calling in ministry and [2] develop plans to fulfill that call.

Bible colleges and seminaries offer essential theological training. However, typically they do not offer the emotional and relational equipping necessary to survive the criticism, sabotage, betrayal, distrust, slander, political maneuverings, coalitions, transference, gossip, power struggles, etc. that exist in every ministry system. Just as a boot camp prepares soldiers for battle, MST 101 helps prepare students for the complex emotional terrain of Christian ministry.

Candidates for MST 101 include: pastors (both at the beginning their careers and for continuing education), youth pastors, seminary and Bible college students, and missionaries. This equipping is proactive, helping pastors and missionaries recognize potential dangers so that they can survive and thrive in ministry, and so that the attrition rate of career ministers can be reduced.

Students may be able to receive college and seminary credits toward their Bachelors, Masters or Doctoral ministry degrees upon successfully completing MST 101. Details are available by accessing the website.

Appendix 5: The Spiritual Space Elevator

Cornerstone Christian Fellowship (West Chester, PA) is actively searching for young men and women who believe they are called to pastor churches or pioneer missionary endeavors. We have adopted a unique paradigm for finding, training, sending and planting — a paradigm that we call the spiritual space elevator.

The Story of the Spiritual Space Elevator

There are many ways a local church can participate in fulfilling the Great Commission. However, in this communication I am setting forth a strategy to reach the nations that I received in July of 2006. At that time, I submitted it to the elders of Cornerstone and we've been dreaming, discussing, praying over it and working towards it ever since.

Here's the story: I was hiking in the Shenandoah National Park in Virginia for three days. At the end of the second day, I came to the campground where I was going to spend the night. Beside the camp store I found a NASA magazine (this definitely caught my eye; I normally don't see a NASA magazine on the Appalachian Trail). The main article was about something called the "space elevator." I turned to the article, and almost as soon as I started reading, I felt a prompting from the Holy Spirit. It was as if the Lord was saying, "Pay attention, this is prophetic. You've been praying for vision. I'm going to use this article to stir you up."

As I tell this story, I am reminded that God can use anything. He can speak through a donkey. He can raise up rocks to sing praises to His name. He can use a NASA magazine. This is why we must keep our eyes open and pay attention!

The article was describing a new idea in space travel. It explained that when the Space Shuttle Columbia lifted off for the first time on April 12, 1981, the dream of a reusable spacecraft was realized. Since then, NASA has launched more than 100 missions, but the price tag of space missions has changed little. The cost of a launch is approximately $10,000 per pound.

For one hundred missions, the space shuttle has been launched into space in the same way: strapped to a rocket and blasted through earth's atmosphere. The goal is achieved—the space shuttle is blasted into space—but it takes tremendous force, there is incredible danger, there is waste (the rocket falls back to earth), and there is a huge price tag for each launch.

Is there another way? Enter the idea of the space elevator.

Imagine a ribbon, a flexible but incredibly strong tube anchored to an offshore sea platform that stretches to a small counterweight approximately 62,000 miles into space. The ribbon would be taut. The counterweight would be in geo-synchronous orbit. Mechanical lifters would then climb the ribbon, carrying cargo and humans into space, at a price of only about $100 to $400 per pound (compared to the normal rocket launch costing approximately $10,000 per pound).

As I was staring at an artist's depiction of what the space elevator might look like, I heard the Lord ask: "Do you understand what I am saying to you? You and your church dream of sending people into the mission field; you long to fulfill the Great Commission. You've been strapping people to rockets. There is another way. Build a spiritual space elevator. Build a center that specifically calls, trains and sends people to pastor new churches and initiate new mission endeavors around the world."

Are you interested in finding out more about this unique 24-month mentoring program that we call the spiritual space elevator? Go to www.spiritualspaceelevator.com.

Appendix 6: Recommendations for Your Library

Favorites and Most Used

Bickle, Mike. Growing in the Prophetic. Lake Mary, Fl.: Creation House.

Clouse & Clouse. Women in Ministry. Downers Grove: Inter-Varsity Press.

Cooke, Graham. A Divine Confrontation. Shippensburg, Pa.: Destiny Image Publishers, Inc.

Cymbala, Jim. Fresh Wind, Fresh Fire. Grand Rapids: Zondervan.

Fee, Gordon & Stuart, Douglas. How to Read the Bible for All It's Worth (Zondervan Publishing).

Edersheim, Alfred. The Life and Times of Jesus the Messiah. Mclean, Va: Macdonald Publishing.

Foster, Richard. Celebration of Discipline. San Francisco: Harper & Row.

Johnston, Robert K. Evangelicals at an Impasse. Atlanta: John Knox Press.

Marshall, Paul. Their Blood Cries Out. Dallas: Word Publishing.

Martin, Walter, R. The Kingdom of the Cults. Minneapolis: Bethany House Publishers.

Nee, Watchman. The Normal Christian Life. New York: Christian Fellowship Publishers, Inc.

Packer, J. I. Knowing God. Downers Grove: Inter-Varsity Press.

Sider, Ronald. Rich Christians in an Age of Hunger. Downers Grove: Inter-Varsity Press.

Snyder, Howard. <u>The Community of the King</u>. Downers Grove: Inter-Varsity Press.

Wurmbrand, Richard & John Piper & Milton Martin, <u>The Triumphant Church</u>. Voice of the Martyrs, Bartlesville, OK.

Yun. <u>The Heavenly Man.</u> London: Monarch Books.

Reference Books — I recommend that you develop your resource library throughout your ministry. I am thankful for some of the wonderful computer resources available, but I have found that books are often more accessible in the realm of study. There are dozens of wonderful possibilities in each category; I am simply offering a few suggestions of where you might start with your library.

Dictionaries and Encyclopedias

Buttrick, George, ed. <u>The Interpreters Dictionary of the Bible</u> (5 volumes), Nashville: Abingdon Press. *(Of the two sets mentioned—this introduces a more scholarly approach and is more exhaustive in scope.)*

Tenney, Merrill, ed. <u>The Zondervan Pictorial Encyclopedia of the Bible</u> (5 volumes),. Grand Rapids: Zondervan. *(This set is less expensive than the Interpreters Dictionary and is well-researched.)*

Language Helps — Besides a good Greek New Testament, Septuagint and Hebrew Old Testament (and lexicons for both languages), two wonderful and consistently used resources in my library are

Kittles (no surprise here for the Greek student) and Sakae Kubo's work listed below.

Aland, Kurt, eds. et al. <u>The Greek New Testament.</u> West Germany: Biblia-Druck GmbH Stuttgart.

Brown, Francis, Driver and Briggs. <u>The New Brown, Driver, Briggs, Gesenius Hebrew and English Lexicon.</u> Peabody, Mass: Hendrickson Publishers, Inc.

Elliger, K. and Rudolph, W., eds. <u>Biblia herbraica Stuttgartensia</u>: Stuttgart: Deutsche Bibelgesellschaft.

Kittel, Gerhard, ed. <u>Theological Dictionary of the New Testament</u>. Grand Rapids: Eerdmans.

Marshall, Reverend Alfred. <u>The NIV Interlinear Greek-English New Testament,</u> Grand Rapids: Zondervan.

Metzger, Bruce M. <u>A Textual Commentary on the Greek New Testament.</u> .New York: United Bible Societies.

Rahlfs, Alfred, ed. <u>Septuaginta.</u> Germany: Biblia-Druck Stuttgart.

Thayer, Joesph Henry. <u>A Greek English Lexicon of the New Testament,</u> Grand Rapids: Zondervan.

Sakae Kubo. <u>A Reader's Greek-English Lexicon of the New Testament</u>. Grand Rapids: Zondervan.

Commentaries — I recommend that you own one scholarly commentary set (the <u>Word Biblical Commentary</u> or <u>The New International Commentary on the New Testament</u> are two good ones). I would also make an immediate purchase of Barclay's New Testament series and Keil &

Delitzsch for the Old Testament. Over time, add one commentary for each book of the Bible. In order to make these particular selections, resource Fee & Douglas' book, How to Read the Bible for All It's Worth (Zondervan Publishing); the authors list their recommendations for commentaries for every book of the Bible in an appendix. This is an extremely helpful list that is well researched and organized.

Albright, Wm. & Freedman, David, eds. The Anchor Bible. New York: Doubleday.

Barclay, William. The Daily Study Bible Series. Phila: Westminster Press.

Bruce, F.F. The New International Commentary on the New Testament. Grand Rapids: Eerdmans Publishing.

Buttrick, George Arthur, The Interpreter's Bible. New York: Abingdon Press.

Clements, Ronald & Black, Matthew, eds. New Century Bible Commentary. Grand Rapids: Eerdmans Publishing.

Gaebelein, Frank E., ed. The Expositor's Bible Commentary. Grand Rapids: Zondervan.

Hubbard, David A., Barker, Glenn W., eds. Word Biblical Commentary. Waco: Word Books.

Keil & Delitzsch, Commentary on the Old Testament. Peabody, Ma: Hendrickson publishers.

Morris, Rev. Canon Leon, ed. The Tyndale New Testament Commentaries. Grand Rapids: Eerdmans.

Osborne, Grant, ed. <u>Life Application Bible Commentary</u>. Wheaton: Tyndale House Publishers.

History — I recommend purchasing Philip Schaff's series and Freeman's book (or one that's similar) right away. Then, in time, you can add to your library.

Bright, John, <u>A History of Israel</u>. Phila: Westminster Press.

Freeman, James M. Manners and Customs of the Bible. Plainfield, NJ: Logos International

Schaff, Philip, <u>History of the Christian Church.</u> Grand Rapids: Eerdmans Publishing.

Whiston, Wm., trans. <u>The Works of Josephus.</u> Peabody, Ma: Hendrickson Publishers.

Apologetics and Evangelism

Ankerberg, John & Weldon, John. <u>Encyclopedia of New Age Beliefs.</u> Eugene, Oregon: harvest House Publishers.

Green Michael. <u>Evangelism Through the Local Church.</u> Nashville: Thomas Nelson Publishers..

Martin, Walter, R. <u>The Kingdom of the Cults.</u> Minneapolis: Bethany House Publishers.

McDowell, Josh. <u>Evidence that Demands a Verdict</u> (Campus Crusade for Christ).

Zachaarias, Ravi, <u>Can man Live Without God.</u> Dallas: Word Publishing.

Counseling

Frost, Jack. Experiencing Father's Embrace. Conway, SC: Father's House Productions, 2002.

Gardner, Thom, Healing the Wounded Heart. Shippensburg, Pa: Destiny Image Publishers, Inc., 2005.

Gurman, Alan & Kniskern, David, Eds. Handbook of Family Therapy (Vol.1 & 2).NY: Brunner/Mazel, Publishers. 1981.

McGoldrick, Monica & Gerson, Randy. Genograms in Family Assessment. NY: W.W. Norton & Company, 1985.

Tripp, Paul David, Instruments in the Redeemer's Hands. Phillipsburg, NJ: P&R Publishing Co, 2002.

Vande Kemp, Hendrika, Ed. Family Therapy: Christian Perspectives. Baker Book House Company, 1991.

Justice and Mission

Costas, Orlando. Christ Outside the Gate. Maryknoll, NY: Orbis Books, 1982.

Haugen, Gary. Good News about Injustice. Downers Grove, Il: InterVarsity Press, 1999.

Scott, Waldron, Bring Forth Justice. Grand Rapids: Eerdmans Publishing.

Sider, Ronald, Just Generosity. Grand Rapids: Baker Books.

Sider, Ronald. Rich Christians in an Age of Hunger. Downers Grove: Inter-Varsity Press.

Winter, Ralph & Hawthorne, Steven, eds. Perspectives. William Carey Library, 1981.

Leadership

Hybels, Bill. <u>Courageous leadership</u>. Grand Rapids: Zondervan.

Richards, Lawrence O. & Hoeldtke, Clyde. <u>Church Leadership</u>. Grand Rapids: Zondervan.

Prayer

Cymbala, Jim. <u>Fresh Wind, Fresh Fire.</u> Grand Rapids: Zondervan.

Foster, Richard. <u>Prayer.</u> Harper SanFrancisco Publishers, 1992.

Olukoya, Dr. D.K. <u>Prayer Rain.</u> Lagos, Nigeria: MFM Ministries.

Warfare

Anderson, Neil T. & Towns, Elmer L. <u>Rivers of Revival.</u> Ventura, Ca: Regal.

Pastoral Ministry Helps — A Christian wedding planner is helpful (examples of vows, ring ceremony, call to worship, etc) as is a funeral manual. If you offer child dedications, a name book like the one below is a necessary addition to your library. For ceremonies: baptisms, weddings and funerals—make use of hymnals of the various denominations. Some beautiful prayers and liturgical structures are available there.

Austin, Dorothea Austin, <u>The Name Book.</u> Minneapolis: Tethany House Publishers

Biddle, Perry H., Jr. <u>A Funeral Manual.</u> Grand Rapids: Eerdmans Publishing.

The Book of Common Prayer. New York: Oxford University Press.

Muzzy, Ruth & Hughes, Kent, The Christian Wedding Planner. Wheaton: Tyndale House Publishers.

For Practical Discipleship

Foster, Richard. Celebration of Discipline. San Fransisco: Harper & Row.

McDowell, Josh. More Than a Carpenter. Carol Stream, Ill: Tyndale House Publishers.

Endnotes

Prologue
Focus on the Family, 1998.
[2] John Mark Ministries, 2008.
[3] Youth With a Mission (YWAM), 2007.
[4] www.parsonage.org (website of Focus on the Family Ministries)

Key 1
[5] Chasteen, John. "Is Your Pastor Burned Out?" Hey Coach John. 10 January, 2008. http://www.heycoachjohn.com/hey_coach_john/2008/01/is-your-pastor.html.
[6] Wilderness can mean different things for different people. I have found tremendous encouragement from walking portions of the Appalachian Trail; you may have a garden to which you can retreat, or a park. The point is: get away from your routine and into nature.
[7] Eldredge, John. Wild at Heart: Discovering the Secret of a Man's Soul. Nashville: Thomas Nelson, 2001,1.

[8] I first heard the term "mind-skin" from a teaching offered by Lance Wallnau.

[9] Hybels, Bill. Courageous Leadership. Grand Rapids: Zondervan, 2002, 29.

[10] Foster, Richard. Celebration of Discipline. San Francisco: Harper & Row.

Key 2

[11] Crone, David. Decisions that Define Us. Brilliant, 1999, 26.

[12] Millard, Candice. The River of Doubt: Theodore Roosevelt's Darkest Journey. New York: Broadway, 2005, 252.

[13] Lewis, C.S. 'Til We Have Faces. Orlando: Harcourt. 1956, 292.

[14] Missionaries must keep this in mind also. A particular ministry conviction may cost you some of your monthly support.

Key 3

[15] Lewis, C.S. The Screwtape Letters. New York: Harper Collins, 1942, 3.

[16] John of the Cross. "Living Flame of Love." Stanza 3

[17] See Appendix 6 for excellent titles on spiritual warfare that will aid you in this.

Key 4

[18] Shelley, Marshall. Renewing Your Church Through Vision and Planning. Minneapolis: Bethany, 1997, 265-266.

[19] The Voice of the Martyrs. <u>The Triumphant Church: A Three-Part Study from the Writings of Richard Wurmbrand, John Piper, and Milton Martin</u>. Bartlesville: VOM, 1999, 4.

[20] Bevere, John. <u>The Bait of Satan:</u> Lake Mary: Charisma, 1994, 6.

[21] Lucado, Max. <u>Facing Your Giants</u>. Nashville: W, 2006, 25.

[22] Gardner, Thom. <u>Healing the Wounded Heart: Removing Obstacles to Intimacy with God</u>. Shippensburg: Destiny Image, 2005, 45.

Key 5

[22] Shelley, Marshall. <u>Renewing Your Church Through Vision and Planning</u>. Minneapolis: Bethany, 1997, 44.

[23] Reccord, Bob. <u>Beneath the Surface</u>, Nashville: Broadman & Holman, 2002.

[24] Means, Patrick. <u>Men's Secret Wars</u>. Grand Rapids: Fleming H. Revell, 1996.

[25] Every church member has a responsibility to test the preaching and the integrity of the Pastor, but we are called to enter a biblical process of discovery and offer our perspectives with humility.

Key 6

[26] Johnson, David & VanVonderen, Jeff. <u>The Subtle Power of Spiritual Abuse</u>. Grand Rapids: Bethany, 1991, 20-21.

Key 7

27 Shelley, Marshall. <u>Renewing Your Church Through Vision and Planning</u>. Minneapolis: Bethany, 1997, 15.

28 Cymbala, Jim. <u>Fresh Wind, Fresh Fire</u>. Grand Rapids: Zondervan, 1997.

29 Stott, John. <u>Between Two Worlds: The Challenge of Preaching Today</u>. London: Hodder & Stoughton, 1982.

30 An excellent book on this subject is *How to Read the Bible for All It's Worth* by Gordon Fee & Douglas Stuart.

31 Peterson, Eugene H. <u>A Long Obedience in the Same Direction: Discipleship in an Instant Society</u>. Downers Grove: InterVarsity, 1980, 159.

32 Shelley, Marshall. <u>Renewing Your Church Through Vision and Planning</u>. Minneapolis: Bethany, 1997, 69.

33 O'Connor, Elizabeth. <u>Journey Inward, Journey Outward</u>. New York: Harper Row, 1968, 131.

Epilogue

34 Foxe, John. <u>Foxe's Book of </u>Martyrs. Whitefish: Kessinger, 2004, 14.

35 Foxe, John. <u>Foxe's Book of </u>Martyrs. Whitefish: Kessinger, 2004, 20.

36 Foxe, John. <u>Foxe's Book of </u>Martyrs. Whitefish: Kessinger, 2004, 24.

37 Wurmbrand, Richard. <u>Tortured for Christ</u>. Bartlesville, Living Sacrifice, 1967, 57.

[38] Peterson, Eugene H. <u>A Long Obedience in the Same Direction: Discipleship in an Instant Society</u>. Downers Grove: InterVarsity, 1980, 92.

Appendix 2

[39] Jackson, Bill. The Quest for the Radical Middle: A History of the Vineyard. Cape Town: Vineyard, 1999, 20.

[40] Peterson, Eugene H. <u>A Long Obedience in the Same Direction: Discipleship in an Instant Society</u>. Downers Grove: InterVarsity, 1980, 25.

Appendix 3

[40] The kerygma is the compiled, major doctrines preached by the Apostles in the New Testament.

Acknowledgements

A part from some very special people in my life, this book would have never been written. Special thanks to Joni, my partner in marriage and soul mate and for Christie and Dana (my daughter and son) — thank you for your encouragement and support. I love you!

Lucinda Sutton, you provided tremendous editorial support and guidance and remained in the trenches with me. This book is better written because of your prayerful skill and artistry with words! Randy Frame, you came along side of me when few people believed in me. Your guidance and experience was invaluable! Phil Bruner, your sketches are inspirational! Thank you for joining me in this venture to encourage pastors and missionaries around the world. Brian McCloskey, thank you for serving with your creative skills and joining me in birthing a ministry.

To the elders and congregation of Cornerstone Christian Fellowship: I have the greatest church family in the whole world. Your prayers, encouragement, and friendships have inspired me to dream big dreams for the Kingdom of God.

I am indebted to my mentors: Dr. Manfred Brauch, Dr.'s Peter and Carol Schreck, and Dr. Glenn Koch.

I am dedicating this book to pastors and missionaries on the front lines. Stand strong! I believe in you and am thankful for your ministry to the Body of Christ.

Biographical Information

Robert Stephen Miller received a Bachelor of Science degree in Physics from Muhlenberg College, a Masters of Divinity degree and a Doctor of Ministry degree in Marriage & Family Ministry from Palmer Seminary. Dr. Miller recently received the Orlando E. Costas Award for Mentoring (Palmer Seminary, 2007) and is passionate about seeing the next generation succeed in ministry. He currently serves as pastor of Cornerstone Christian Fellowship (the church he helped to establish in 1989), is president of the Identity School for Christian Ministry (a school focused on preparing pastors and missionaries navigate the emotional terrain of ministry), and is currently constructing what he calls a *spiritual space*

elevator (a new paradigm of training, sending and planting for the Kingdom of God).

Dr. Robert S. Miller
Cornerstone Christian Fellowship
426 W. Gay St. West Chester, PA 19380

9 781606 479773